TAKE THE LAW INTO YOUR OWN HANDS™

P9-CRJ-015

How to Form a Simple Corporation in Texas

With Forms

Karen Ann Rolcik*
Mark Warda†
Attorneys at Law

*Admitted to practice in Texas
†Admitted to practice in Florida

SPHINX PUBLISHING
Sphinx International, Inc.
1725 Clearwater-Largo Rd., S.
Post Office Box 2005
Clearwater, FL 34617
Tel: (813) 587-0999

SPHINX®
is a registered trademark of Sphinx International, Inc.

> Note: The law changes constantly and is sub-
> ject to different interpretations. It is up to you
> to check it thoroughly before relying on it.
> Neither the author nor the publisher guaran-
> tees the outcome of the uses to which this
> material is put.

First Edition, 1995

ISBN 1-57248-009-2
Library of Congress Catalog Number: 94-74096

Manufactured in the United States of America.

This publication is designed to provide accurate and authoritative information in regard to the subject matter covered. It is sold with the understanding that the publisher is not engaged in rendering legal, accounting or other professional services. If legal advice or other expert assistance is required, the service of a competent professional person should be sought.

> -From a Declaration of Principles jointly adopted by a Committee of the American Bar Association and a Committee of Publishers.

Published by Sphinx Publishing, a division of Sphinx International, Inc., Post Office Box 25, Clearwater, Florida 34617-0025. This publication is available by mail for $19.95 plus $3.50 shipping. For credit card orders call 1-800-226-5291.

Table of Contents

Introduction

Each year hundreds of thousands of corporations are registered in this country, tens of thousands in Texas alone. The corporation is the preferred way of doing business for most people because it offers many advantages over partnerships and sole proprietorships. It is not a coincidence that the largest businesses in the world are corporations.

The main reason people incorporate is to avoid personal liability. While sole proprietors and partners have all of their personal assets at risk, corporate shareholders risk only what they paid for their stock. With so many people ready to sue for any reason or for no reason, the corporation is one of the few inexpensive protections left.

Creating a simple corporation is very easy and it is the purpose of this book to explain, in simple language, how you can do it yourself. A simple corporation as used in this book is one in which there are five or fewer shareholders and all of them are active in the business. If you plan to sell stock to someone who is not active in the business or to have six or more shareholders, you should seek the advice of an attorney. However, some guidance is provided throughout this book as to what some of the concerns will be in these circumstances.

If your situation is in any way complicated or involves factors not mentioned in this book, you should seek the advice of an attorney practicing corporate law. The cost of a short consultation can be a lot cheaper than the consequences of violating the law.

If you plan to sell stock to outside investors, you should consult with a lawyer who specializes in securities laws. Selling a few thousand shares of stock to friends and neighbors may sound like an easy way to raise capital for your business, but it is not! Since the stock market crash of the 1930s there have been federal laws regulating the sale of securities. There are harsh criminal penalties for violators and the laws don't have many loopholes. The basic rules are explained in Chapter 5.

This book also explains the basics of corporate taxation, but you should discuss your own particular situation with your accountant before deciding what is best for you. He or she can also set you up with an efficient system of bookkeeping which can save both time and money.

Good luck with your new business!

8

Using Self-Help Law Books

Whenever you shop for a product or service, you are faced with various levels of quality and price. In deciding upon which product or service to buy, you make a cost/value analysis based upon what you are willing to pay and the quality you desire.

When buying a car you decide whether you want transportation, comfort, status, or sex appeal. Accordingly, you decide among such choices as a Chevette, a Lincoln, a Rolls Royce, or a Porsche. Before making a decision, you usually weigh the merits of each option against the cost.

When you get a headache, you can take a pain reliever (such as aspirin) or go visit a medical specialist for a neurological examination. Given this choice, most people, of course, take a pain reliever, since it only costs pennies, whereas a medical examination would cost hundreds of dollars and take a lot of time. This is usually a very logical choice because very rarely is anything more than a pain reliever needed for a headache. But in some cases, a headache may indicate a brain tumor, and failing to see a specialist right away can result in complications. Should everyone with a headache go to a specialist? Of course not. But people treating their own illnesses must realize that they are taking a chance, and based upon their cost/value analysis of the situation, they are taking the most logical option.

The same cost/value analysis must be made in deciding to do one's own legal work. Many legal situations are very straight forward, requiring a simple form and no complicated analysis. Anyone with a little intelligence and a book of instructions can handle the matter without outside help.

But there is always the chance that complications are involved which only an attorney would notice. To simplify the law into a book like this, often numerous legal cases must be condensed into a single sentence or paragraph. Otherwise, the book would be several hundred pages long and too complicated for most people. However, this simplification necessarily leaves out many details and nuances which would apply to special or unusual situations. Also, there are many ways to interpret most legal questions. Your case may come before a judge who disagrees with the analysis of our author.

Therefore, in deciding to use a self-help law book and to do your own legal work, you must realize that you are making a cost/value analysis and deciding that the chance your case will not turn out to your satisfaction is outweighed by the money you will save in doing it yourself. Most people addressing their own simple legal matters will probably never have a problem. But occasionally someone may find that it ended up costing them more to have an attorney straighten out the situation than it would have if they had hired an attorney to begin with.

Chapter 1
What is a Corporation?

A corporation is a legal "person" which can be created under state law. As a person, a corporation has certain rights and obligations such as the right to do business and the obligation to pay taxes. Sometimes one hears of a law referring to "natural persons." These references differentiate humans from corporations, which are persons, but not natural persons.

Business corporations were invented hundreds of years ago to promote risky ventures. Prior to the use of corporations, persons engaged in business faced the possibility of unlimited liability. By using a corporation, many people could put up a fixed sum of money for a new venture such as a voyage to explore the new world. If the venture made money they shared the profits. If the venture got into debt, the most they could lose was the initial investment they put up.

The reasons for having a corporation are the same today. Corporations allow investors to put up money for new ventures without risk of further liability. While our legal system is making more and more people liable for more and more things, the corporation remains one of the few innovations which has not yet been abandoned.

Before forming a corporation you should be familiar with these common corporate terms which will be used throughout the text:

A **shareholder** is a person who owns stock in a corporation. In most small corporations the shareholders are the same as the officers and directors, but in large corporations most shareholders are not officers or directors. Sometimes small corporations have shareholders who are not officers, such as when the stock is in one spouse's name and the other spouse runs the business. Specific laws regarding issuance of shares and shareholders' rights are in the Texas Business Corporation Act ("TBCA"), articles 2.12 through 2.30.

Officers are usually the president, secretary, treasurer and vice president. These persons run the day-to-day affairs of the business. They are elected each year by a vote of the board of directors. In Texas one person can hold all of the offices of a corporation.

The **board of directors** is the controlling body of a corporation which makes major corporate decisions and elects the officers. It usually meets just once a year. A corporation can have one director (who can also hold all offices and own all stock). In a small corporation the board members are usually also officers.

The **registered agent** is the person designated by the corporation to receive legal papers which must be served on the corporation. The registered agent should be regularly available at the **registered office** of the corporation. The registered office can be the corporate office or the office of the corporation's attorney or other person who is the registered agent.

Articles of Incorporation is the name of the document which is filed with the Secretary of State to start the corporation. In most cases it legally needs to contain only eight basic statements. Some corporations have lengthy articles of incorporation, but this just makes it harder to make changes in the corporate structure. It is usually better to keep the articles short and put the details in the bylaws.

Bylaws are the rules governing the structure and operation of the corporation. Typically the bylaws will set out rules for the board of directors, officers, shareholders and corporate formalities.

The **Texas Business Corporation Act** contains most of Texas' laws regarding general corporate activities. For example, it lists all of the powers of corporations so they do not have to be recited again in the articles or bylaws. Articles of TBCA will be referred to throughout the text like this: "art. 2.01."

Legal definitions of other corporate terms are included in TBCA art. 1.01 contained in Appendix A.

Chapter 2

Should You Incorporate?

Before forming a corporation the business owner or prospective business owner should become familiar with the advantages and disadvantages of incorporating.

Advantages

The following are some of the advantages that a corporation has over other forms of businesses such as sole proprietorships and partnerships.

Limited Liability

The main reason for forming a corporation is to limit the liability of the owners. In a sole proprietorship or partnership the owners are personally liable for the debts and liabilities of the business, and creditors can go after all of their assets to collect. If a corporation is formed and operated properly, the owners can be protected from all such liability.

Examples:

1.   If several people are in partnership and one of them makes many large extravagant purchases in the name of the partnership, the other partners can be held liable for the full amount of all such purchases. The creditors can take the bank accounts, cars, real estate and other property of any partner to pay the debts of the partnership. If only one partner has money, he or she may have to pay all of the debts run up by all the other partners. When doing business in the corporate

form, the corporation may go bankrupt and the shareholders may lose their initial investment, but the creditors cannot touch the assets of the owners.

2.   If a person runs a taxi business and one of the drivers causes a terrible accident, the owner can be held liable for the full amount of the damages. If the taxi driver was on drugs and killed several people and the damages amount to millions of dollars more than the insurance coverage, the owner may lose everything he has. With a corporation, only the corporation would be liable, and if there was not enough money the owner's personal assets still couldn't be touched.

There was once a business owner who owned hundreds of taxis. He put one or two in each of hundreds of different corporations which he owned. Each corporation had only minimum insurance, and when one taxi was involved in an accident the owner lost only the assets of that corporation.

But Note: If a corporate officer or shareholder does something negligent himself, or signs a debt personally, or guarantees a corporate debt, the corporation will not protect him from the consequences of his own act or from the debt. Also, if a corporation does not follow the proper corporate formalities it may be ignored by a court and the owners or officers may be held personally liable. The formalities include having separate bank accounts, holding meetings, and keeping minutes. When a court ignores a corporate structure and holds the owners or officers liable it is called **piercing the corporate veil**. A good explanation of Texas law on piercing the corporate veil is contained in the Texas Supreme Court case, *Castleberry v. Branscum*, 721 SW2d 270 (1986).

Continuous Existence

A corporation may have a perpetual existence. When a sole proprietor or partner dies, the assets of their business may go to their heirs but the business does not exist any longer. If the surviving spouse or other heirs of a business owner want to continue the business in their own names, they will be considered a new business even if they are using the assets of the old business. With a partnership, the death of one partner may cause a dissolution of the business.

Examples:

1.   If a person dies owning a sole proprietorship, his or her spouse may want to continue the business. That person may inherit all of the assets but will have to start a new business. This means getting new licenses and tax numbers, registering the name and establishing credit from scratch. With a corporation, the business continues with all of the same licenses, bank accounts, etc.

2.   If one partner dies, the partnership may be forced out of business. The heirs of the deceased partner can force the sale of their share of the assets of the partnership even if the surviving partner needs them to continue the business.

If he does not have the money to buy the heirs out, the business may have to be dissolved. With a corporation, the heirs would only inherit stock. With properly drawn documents the business could continue.

Ease of Transferability

A corporation and all of its assets and accounts may be transferred by the simple assignment of a stock certificate. With a sole proprietorship or partnership, each of the individual assets must be transferred and the accounts, licenses, and permits must be individually transferred.

Example:

If a sole proprietorship is sold, the new owner will have to get a new occupational license, set up his own bank account and apply for a new taxpayer identification number. The title to any vehicles and real estate will have to be put in his name and all open accounts will have to be changed to his name. He will probably have to submit new credit applications. With a corporation, all of these items remain in the same corporate name. As the new shareholder he would elect himself director, and as director he would elect himself president, treasurer, and any other offices he wanted to hold.

Note: In some cases, the new owners will have to submit personal applications for such things as credit lines or liquor licenses.

Ownership Can Be Transferred Without Control

By distributing stock the owner of a business can share the profits of a business without giving up control.

Example:

If a person wants to give his children some of the profits of his business, he can give them stock and pay dividends to them without giving them any control over the management. This would not be practical with a partnership or sole proprietorship.

Ease of Raising Capital

A corporation may raise capital by selling stock or borrowing money. A corporation does not pay taxes on money it raises by the sale of stock.

Example:

If a corporation wants to expand, the owners can sell off 10%, 50%, or 90% of the stock and still remain in control of the business. The people putting up the money may be more willing to invest if they know they will have a piece of the action than if they were making a loan with a limited return. They may not want to become partners in a partnership.

Note: There are strict rules about the sale of stock with criminal penalties and monetary fines up to $100,000. See Chapter 5.

Separate Record Keeping

A corporation has its own bank accounts and records. A partner or sole proprietor may have trouble differentiating which of his expenses were for business and which were for personal items.

Tax Advantages

There are some tax advantages which are available only to corporations.

Examples:

1. Medical insurance for your family may be fully deductible.

2. A tax deferred trust can be set up for a retirement plan.

3. Losses are fully deductible for a corporation whereas an individual must prove there was a profit motive before deducting losses.

Ease of Estate Planning

With a corporation, shares of a company can be distributed more easily than with a partnership. Different heirs can be given different percentages and control can be limited to those heirs deemed appropriate.

Prestige

The name of a corporation sounds more prestigious than the name of a sole proprietor to some people. John Smith d/b/a Acme Builders sounds like one lone guy. Acme Builders, Incorporated, sounds like it might be a large operation. No one needs to know that it is run out of a garage. One female writer on the subject has suggested that a woman who is president of a corporation looks more successful than one doing business in her own name. This probably applies to everyone.

Separate Credit Rating

A corporation has its own credit rating, which can be better or worse than the owner's credit rating. A corporate business can go bankrupt while the owner's credit remains unaffected, or an owner's credit may be bad but the corporation may maintain a good rating.

Disadvantages

Extra Tax Return

A corporation is required to file its own tax return. This is a bit longer and more complicated than the form required by a sole proprietorship and may entail additional expenses if the services of an accountant are required. A partnership must also file its own tax return so there is no advantage or disadvantage over a partnership as far as tax returns are concerned.

Annual Report

A corporation must file a one-page annual report with the state (which lists names and addresses of officers and directors).

Separate Records

The owners of a corporation must be careful to keep their personal business separate from the business of the corporation. The corporation must have its own records and have minutes of meetings. Money must be kept separate. But in every business, records should be kept separate, so the corporate structure might make it easier to do so.

Extra Expenses

There are, of course, expenses in operating a corporation compared to not operating one. People who employ an attorney to form their corporation pay a lot more than people who use this book. A corporation owner will have to pay unemployment compensation for himself which he wouldn't have to pay as a sole proprietor. The state unemployment tax starts at 2.7% of the first $9000 ($243 per year). If there are no claims, the rate drops.

Checking Accounts

Checks made out to a corporation cannot be cashed; they must be deposited into a corporate account. Some banks have higher fees just for incorporated businesses. See page 38 for tips on avoiding high bank fees.

Chapter 3
What Type of Corporation is Best?

Texas Corporation or Foreign Corporation

A person wishing to form a corporation must decide whether the corporation will be a Texas corporation or a "foreign" corporation. A **foreign corporation** is one incorporated in another state which does business in Texas. In the past, there was some advantage to incorporating in Delaware, since that state had very liberal laws regarding corporations, and many national corporations are incorporated there. There are books on the market (the most prominent being published in Delaware) which advise readers to incorporate there. Others suggest other states such as Nevada. However, in most cases it is more advantageous for a Texas business to incorporate in Texas.

Today Texas has very favorable corporate laws, so out-of-state laws are not an advantage. If you form a corporation in a state other than Texas, you will have to have an agent or an office in that state and will have to register as a foreign corporation doing business in Texas. This is more expensive and more complicated than just registering as a Texas corporation to begin with.

S-corporation or C-corporation

A corporation has a choice of how it wants to be taxed. It can make the election at the beginning of its existence or at the beginning of a new tax year. The choices are as follows:

S-corporation

Sometimes called a "Subchapter S corporation," an S-corporation pays no income tax and may only be used for small businesses. All of the income or losses of the corporation for the year are passed through to the shareholders, who report them on their individual returns. At the end of each year the corporation files an "information return" listing all of its income, expenses, depreciation, etc., and sends to each shareholder a Form K-1, which is notice of his or her share as determined by percentage of stock ownership. These amounts are then listed on the shareholder's 1040 tax return.

Advantages. Using this method avoids double taxation and allows pass-through of losses and depreciation. The business is treated like a partnership. Since many businesses have tax losses during the first years due to start-up costs, many businesses elect "S" status and switch over to C-corporation status in later years. Once a corporation terminates its "S" status, there is a five year waiting period before it can switch back.

Disadvantages. If shareholders are in high income brackets, their share of the profits will be taxed at those rates. Shareholders who do not "materially participate" in the business cannot deduct losses. Some fringe benefits such as health and life insurance may not be tax deductible in an S-corporation.

Requirements. To qualify for S-corporation status the corporation must:

•have no more than 35 shareholders, none of whom are non-resident aliens or corporations, all of whom consent to the election (shares owned by a husband and wife jointly are considered owned by one shareholder)

•have only one class of stock

•not be a member of an "affiliated group"

•generate at least 20% of its income in this country and have no more than 20% of its income from "passive" sources (interest, rents, dividends, royalties, securities transactions)

•file Form 2553 before the end of the 15th day of the third month of the tax year for which it is to be effective and have it approved by the IRS.

Multiple Corporations. The IRS has approved the use of two or more S-corporations in partnership to increase the number of allowable investors in a venture. It may also be possible for an S-corporation to form a partnership with a C-corporation.

C-corporation

A C-corporation pays taxes on its net earnings at corporate tax rates. Salaries of officers, directors and employees are deducted from income so are not taxed to the corporation, but money paid out in dividends is taxed twice. It is taxed at the corporation's rate as part of its profit, and then the shareholders must include the amounts they receive as dividends in their income.

Advantages. If taxpayers are in a higher tax bracket than the corporation and the money will be left in the company for expansion, taxes are saved. Fringe benefits such as health, accident, and life insurance are deductible expenses.

Disadvantages. Double taxation of dividends by the federal government is the biggest problem with a C-corporation. Also, Texas has a franchise tax which comes very close to being an income tax on corporations. The franchise tax is a combination of a tax imposed on "capital" and a tax imposed on "earned surplus" (a disguised income tax). The franchise tax on capital is imposed at a rate of 0.25%. The franchise tax on "earned surplus" is imposed at a rate of 4.5%. Franchise tax must be reported on the Texas Corporation Tax Report form and paid May 15th. **Note:** This tax does not apply to money taken out as salaries, and many small business owners take all profits out as salaries to avoid double taxation and the Texas franchise tax. But there are rules requiring that salaries be reasonable and if a shareholder's salary is deemed to be too high, relative to his or her job, the salary may be considered dividends and subject to the double taxation.

Requirements. None. All corporations are C-corporations unless they specifically elect to become S-corporations.

Inc. or P.C.

Certain types of services can only be rendered by a corporation if it is a "Professional Corporation." These are businesses such as attorneys, dentists, certified public accountants, veterinarians, nurses, life insurance agents, chiropractors, and similarly licensed professionals. A professional corporation comes under nearly all of the rules of the Texas Business Corporation Act regarding corporations in general unless they conflict with Texas Revised Civil Statutes Annotated article 1528e, commonly known as the Texas Professional Corporation Act ("TPCA"), which specifically governs professional corporations. The major differences between the two are:

Purpose

A professional corporation must have one specific purpose spelled out in the articles of incorporation and that purpose must be to practice one of the professions. It may not engage in any other business, but it may invest its funds in real estate, stocks, bonds, mortgages or other types of investments. A professional corporation may change its purpose to another legal purpose, but it will then no longer be a professional corporation.

Name

The name of a professional corporation must use the words "Company," "Corporation," "Incorporated" or any abbreviation of these, or the phrase "Professional Corporation" or the initials "P.C." It may contain the name of some or all of the shareholders and may contain the names of deceased or retired shareholders, provided the name is not contrary to the law or ethics regulating the practice of the professional service rendered through the professional corporation. (TPCA, Section 8)

Shareholders

Only persons licensed to practice the profession may be shareholders of a professional corporation. A shareholder who loses his or her right to practice must immediately sever all employment with and financial interests in such a corporation.

Merger

A professional corporation may not merge with any other corporation except a Texas professional corporation which is licensed to perform the same type of services.

P.A.

Individuals licensed to practice medicine by the Texas State Board of Medical Examiners (medical doctors and osteopaths) and podiatrists may render services in the form of a corporation if it is a "Professional Association." A professional association comes under many of the rules of the Texas Business Corporation Act regarding corporations in general unless they conflict with Texas Revised Civil Statutes Annotated Article 1528f, commonly known as the Texas Professional Association Act ("TPAA"), which specifically governs profession associations. The major differences between a general corporation and a professional association are:

Purpose

A professional association must have one special purpose spelled out in the articles of association and that purpose must be to engage in the practice of medicine or podiatry. It may not engage in any other business, but it may invest its funds in real estate, mortgages, stocks, bonds or other investments. (TPAA Section 5(A)).

Name

The name of a professional association must include the word or words "Associated," "Association," "Professional Association," or "and Associates," or the abbreviation "Assoc." or "P.A." The name shall not be one that is contrary to or in conflict with any law or ethics regulating the practice or practitioners of any professional service rendered through or in connection with the professional association.

Shareholders

Only persons licensed to practice medicine or podiatry may be members (shareholders).

Chapter 4
Start-up Procedures

Name Check

The very first thing to do before starting a corporation is to thoroughly check out the name you wish to use to be sure it is available. Many business have been forced to stop using their name after spending thousands of dollars promoting it.

Local Records

To check for other corporations using the name you want, you should call the corporations section of the Secretary of State's office at (512) 463-5555. If your name is too similar to another corporate name then you will not be allowed to register it. You should also ask about assumed names. Assumed names are business names being used by individuals and corporations. There is no law saying that two people cannot use the same assumed name, so the Secretary of State allows anyone to file any name, even if a hundred other people already registered it.

Assumed names are registered in the county in which the person is doing business, or, if a corporation, in the county where the entity maintains its registered office and with the Secretary of State. If you want to be sure that no one else has used your name you should check the official records of your county and any other counties where you plan to do business. It is also advisable to check local phone books.

National Records

Occasionally, local businesses will get letters from national companies ordering them to stop using a name that has been registered as a federal trademark. To be sure this will not happen you can have a search done of the records of the trademark office in Washington. If you plan to do business out of state it is especially important to search such records. Some public libraries have computer access to the records of the trademark office and can perform a search for a nominal fee or possibly for free. Another place to check is the *Trade Names Directory,* which is available at many libraries. A more thorough search would include other directories and phone books of major cities. Some companies offer to perform searches of the trademark office and other directories and phone books. The cost is typically $100 or $200. Some search companies are:

Government Liaison Services, Inc.
P. O. Box 10648
Arlington, VA 22209
(703) 524-8200

Thomson & Thomson
500 Victory Road
North Quincy, MA 02171-1545
(800) 692-8833

XL Corporate Service
62 White Street
New York, NY 10013
(800) 221-2972

Name Reservation

It is possible to reserve a name for a corporation for a period of 120 days for a fee of $40. However, this is usually pointless because it is just as easy to file the articles of incorporation as it is to reserve the name. One possible reason for reserving a name would be to hold it while waiting for a trademark name search to arrive.

Similar Names

Sometimes it seems like every good name is taken. But a name can often be modified slightly or used on a different type of goods. If there is a "TriCounty Painting, Inc." in Dallas, it may be possible to use something like "TriCounty Painting of Austin, Inc." if you are in a different part of the state. Try different variations if your favorite is taken. Another possibility is to give the corporation one name and then do business under an assumed name. (See "Assumed Names" on page 28.)

Example:

If you want to use the name "Flowers by Freida" in Houston and there is already a "Flowers by Freida, Inc." in Fort Worth, you might incorporate under the name "Freida Jones, Inc." and then register the corporation as doing business under the fictitious name "Flowers by Freida." Unless "Flowers by Freida, Inc." has registered a trademark for the name either in Texas or nationally, you will probably be able to use the name. **Note:** You should realize that you might run into complications later, especially if you decide to expand into other areas of the state. One protection available would be to register the name as a trademark. This would give you exclusive use of the name anywhere that someone else was not already using it. (See below.)

Forbidden Names

A corporation may not use certain words in its name if there would be a likelihood of confusion. There are state and federal laws which control the use of these words. In most cases, your application will be rejected if you use a forbidden word. Some of the words which may not be used without special licenses or registration are:

Accounting	Cooperative
Bank	Disney
Banker	Insurance
Banking	Olympic
Credit Union	Trust Company

Trademarks

The name of a business cannot be registered as a trademark, but if the name is used in connection with goods or services it may be registered and such registration will grant the holder exclusive rights to use that name except in areas where someone else has already used the name. A trademark may be registered either in Texas or in the entire country.

Each trademark is registered for a certain "class" of goods. If you want to sell "Zapata" chewing gum, it doesn't matter that someone has registered the name "Zapata" for use on shoes. If you want to register the mark for several types of goods or services, you must register it for each different class into which the goods or services fall, and pay a separate fee for each category.

For protection within the state of Texas the mark may be registered with the Texas Trademark Office of the Texas Secretary of State's office. The cost is about $50. Application forms and instructions are contained in the book *How to Start a Business in Texas*, published by Sphinx Publishing or they can be obtained from:

Secretary of State
Statutory Filings Division
Corporations Section
Attn: Trademark Examiner
P.O. Box 13697
Austin, TX 78711
(512) 436-5576

For protection across the entire United States, the mark can be registered with the United States Patent and Trademark Office and the cost is about $200. The procedure for federal registration is more complicated than state registration and is explained in the book *How to Register Your Own Trademark*, available from Sphinx Publishing.

Assumed Names

A corporation may operate under an assumed name just as an individual can. This is done when a corporation wants to operate several businesses under different names or if the business name is not available as a corporate name. Assumed names are generally registered in the county where the corporation has a registered office and with the Secretary of State. However, registering an assumed name does not give the registrant any rights to the name. While corporate names are carefully checked by the Secretary of State and disallowed if they are similar to others, assumed names are filed without checking and any number of people may register the same name. The cost of registering an assumed name is $25. Application forms and instructions are contained in the book *How to Start a Business in Texas*, published by Sphinx Publishing, or they can be obtained from your local courthouse or by writing:

Secretary of State
Statutory Filings Division
Corporations Section
P.O. Box 13697
Austin, TX 78711-3697
(512) 463-5582

Note: When an assumed name is used by a corporation, the corporate name should also be used. If the public does not see that they are dealing with a corporation, they may be able to "pierce the corporate veil" and sue the shareholders individually.

Articles of Incorporation

The act which creates the corporation is the filing of articles of incorporation with the Secretary of State in Austin. Some corporations have long, elaborate articles which spell out numerous powers and functions, but most of this is unnecessary. The powers of corporations are spelled out in Texas law (See TBCA art. 2.02 in Appendix A) and do not have to be repeated. (In fact the statute *says* that the powers do not have to be repeated in the articles, but they often are. Attorneys can charge a lot more for articles of incorporation which are long and look complicated.) The main reason to keep the articles of incorporation short is to avoid having to amend them later. By putting all but the basics in the bylaws of the corporation, you can make changes in the corporate structure much more easily. The articles included in this book (Forms A and B) are as simple as possible for this purpose.

Requirements

Texas law requires that only eight things be included in the articles of incorporation. Some things, such as the regulations for the operation of the corporation, may be spelled out in the articles of incorporation, but this is not advisable since any changes would then require the complicated process of amending the articles. It is better to spell these things out in the bylaws. The eight matters required to be contained in the articles and a few of the optional provisions are:

Name of the corporation. The corporation name *must* include one of the following six words:

Incorporated	Corp.
Inc.	Company
Corporation	Co.

The reason is that persons dealing with the business will be on notice that it is a corporation. This is important in protecting the shareholders from liability. The last two choices, "company" and "co." are not as good as the others because they are not clear notice that the business is incorporated.

Duration The duration of the corporation may be perpetual, a term of years or a date certain.

Purpose The purpose or purposes for which the corporation is organized which may be stated to be, or to include, to transact any and all lawful business for which corporations may be organized under the Texas Business Corporation Act.

The total number of shares of stock the corporation is authorized to issue and the par value of the shares or a statement that the shares are without par value. This is usually an even number such as 100, 1000 or 1,000,000. It doesn't matter what number you pick. A lot of people authorize 1,000,000 shares (with a par value of $0.01 or 0.001) because it sounds impressive.

In some cases, it may be advantageous to issue different classes of stock such as common and preferred or voting and non-voting, but such matters should be discussed with an attorney or accountant.

If there are different classes of stock, the articles of incorporation must contain a designation of the classes, the number of shares in each class, the par value of each class, and a statement of the preferences, limitations and relative rights of each class. In addition, if there are to be any preferred or special shares issued in series, the articles must explain the relative rights and preferences and/or any authority of the board of directors to establish preferences. Any preemptive rights must also be spelled out.

This book will explain how to form a corporation with one class of stock. It is usually advisable to authorize double or quadruple the amount of stock which will be initially issued. The unissued stock can be issued later if more capital is contributed by a shareholder or by a new member of the business.

One important point to keep in mind when issuing stock is that the full par value must be paid for the shares. If this is not done then the shareholder can later be held liable for the full par value. For more important information about issuing stock see Chapter 5.

Commencement of Business. A statement that the corporation will not commence business until it has received for the issuance of shares consideration of the value of a stated sum which shall be at least $1,000.00. "Consideration" can be in the form of money, labor done or property actually received.

The name of the registered agent and the address of the registered office. Each corporation must have a registered agent and a registered office. The registered agent can be any individual or a corporation. The registered office can be the business office of the corporation if the registered agent works out of that office, or it can be the office of another individual who is the registered agent (such as an attorney) or it may be a corporate registered agent's office. The business address of the registered agent is considered the registered office of the corporation. A post office box alone is not a sufficient address for the registered office.

Directors. The number of directors making up the initial board of directors and their names and addresses must be included in the articles of incorporation. The name of the city and state are a sufficient address for the directors.

The name and address of the incorporator of the corporation. This may be any person, even if that person has no future interest in the corporation. For people who need to be incorporated quickly, there are companies in Austin which would, on a moment's notice, have someone sign and run over to the Corporations Section to file corporate articles which are later assigned to the real parties in interest. Only one incorporator is required but every person who is listed as an incorporator must sign the documents. The incorporator does not have to be a resident of Texas.

Professional Corporations. There are two additional requirements for corporations that will be professional corporations (see page 21). These are:

- The purpose of the corporation must be stated and must be limited to the practice of one profession.

- The name must contain the designation "Professional Corporation" or "P.C."

Effective date. A specific effective date may be in the articles but is not required. They are effective upon filing. If an effective date is specified it may not be more than 90 days after filing.

Execution

The articles of incorporation must be signed by each incorporator and dated. The articles do not have to be notarized. Anyone over the age of 18 can be the incorporator, and there is no need to have more than one person sign. Rights of other parties can be spelled out at the incorporation meeting (also known as the organizational meeting).

Forms

Articles of incorporation need not be on any certain form. They can be typed on blank paper or can be on a fill-in-the-blank form. In the back of this book are forms of articles of incorporation for both a regular corporation (Form A) and a professional corporation (Form B).

Filing

The articles of incorporation must be filed with the Secretary of State of Texas by sending them to:

> Corporations Section
> Statutory Filings Division
> Office of the Secretary of State
> P. O. Box 13697
> Austin, TX 78711-3697

You should mail them along with a transmittal letter (Form C) and the filing fees. The filing fee (as of 1995) is $300. If you wish to receive a certified copy of the articles, the cost is $1 per page plus $5 for the certificate. This is an unnecessary expense since such certified copy is rarely, if ever, needed. The better alternative is to enclose a photocopy along with the articles and ask that it be "stamped with the filing date" and returned.

The return time for the articles is usually a week or two. If there is a need to have them back quickly they may be sent by a courier, such as Federal Express, with prepaid return. In such cases they are filed the day received and returned shortly thereafter. The address for courier delivery is:

> Corporations Section
> Office of the Secretary of State
> James Earl Rudder State Office Building
> 1019 Brazos
> Austin, TX 78701

If you want the articles to be reviewed or filed very quickly, you may request "special handling" or "expedited handling." The fee for this service is $10 per document. The documents are sorted when received by the Secretary of State and those requesting special handling or expedited handling are processed prior to all other mail received that day. This $10 fee is also required for documents filed in person which are requested to be given special handling or expedited handling.

Shareholder Agreement

Whenever there are two or more shareholders in a corporation they should consider drawing up a shareholder agreement. This document spells out what is to happen in the event of a disagreement between the shareholders. In closely held corporations the minority shareholders have a risk of being locked into a long term enterprise with little or no way to withdraw their capital. A shareholder agreement is a fairly complicated document and you should consider having it drawn up by an attorney. This may be costly but the expense should be weighed against the costs of lengthy litigation should the shareholders break up. A less expensive alternative is to obtain a few sample agreements from a law library and tailor one to fit your needs. Some of the things which may be addressed in such an agreement are as follows:

> Veto by minority shareholder
> Greater than majority voting requirement
> Cumulative voting
> Deadlocks
> Arbitration
> Dissolution
> Compulsory buy-out
> Preemptive rights
> Restrictions on transfers of shares
> Refusal of a party to participate

Organizational Paperwork

Every corporation must have bylaws and must maintain a set of minutes of its meetings. The bylaws must be adopted at the first meeting and the first minutes of the corporation will be of the organizational meeting.

Bylaws

The bylaws are the rules for organization and operation of the corporation. They are required by TBCA art. 2.23. Two sets of bylaws are included with this book. Form G is for simple corporations and Form H is for professional corporations. To complete either of them you should fill in the name of the corporation, the city of the main office of the corporation, the proposed date of the annual meeting (this can be varied each year as needed), and the number of directors to be on the board.

Waiver of Notice

Before a meeting of the incorporators, the board of directors or the shareholders can be held to transact lawful business, formal notice must be given to the parties ahead of time. Since small corporations often need to have meetings on short notice and do not want to be bothered with formal notices, it is customary to have all parties sign written waivers of notice. Texas law allows the waiver to be signed at any time, even after the meeting has taken place, for both shareholders TBCA art. 9.10 (A) and for directors TBCA art. 9.10 (B). Waivers of notice are included in this book for the organizational meeting (Form E) and for the annual and special meetings (Forms N, P, R, and T)

Minutes

As part of the formal requirements of operating a corporation, minutes must be kept of the meetings of shareholders and the board of directors. Usually only one meeting of each is required per year (the annual meeting) unless there is some special need for a meeting in the interim (such as the resignation of an officer). The first minutes that will be needed are the minutes of the organizational meeting of the corporation. At this meeting the officers and directors are elected; the bylaws, corporate seal and stock certificates are adopted; and other organizational decisions made. Most of the forms should be self-explanatory, but sample filled-out forms are in Appendix B of this book.

Resolutions

When the board of directors or shareholders make major decisions it is usually done in the form of a resolution. At the organizational meeting the important resolutions are those choosing a bank (Form I) and adopting S-corporation status (Form M).

Consent in Lieu of Organizational Meeting

Texas law (TBCA art. 3.06 and 9.10) allows the initial board of directors to execute incorporation papers without a meeting, but it is better to have a formal meeting to prove to possible future creditors that you conducted the corporation in a formal manner.

Tax Forms

Form SS-4 (Employer Identification Number)

Prior to opening a bank account the corporation must obtain a "taxpayer identification number," which is the corporate equivalent of a social security number. This is done by filing Form SS-4, included in this book as Form D. This usually takes two or three weeks, so it should be filed early. Send the form to:

Internal Revenue Service Center
Austin, TX 73301

If you need the number quickly you may be able to obtain the number by phone by calling the IRS at (512) 462-7843 before 2:30 p.m. Be sure to have your SS-4 form complete and in front of you before calling.

When you apply for this number you will probably be put on the mailing list for other corporate tax forms. If you do not receive these, you should call your local IRS forms number and request the forms for new businesses. These include Circular E, explaining the taxes due, the W-4 forms for each employee, the tax deposit coupons, and Form 941 the quarterly return for withholding.

Form 2553 (S-corporation)

If your corporation is to be taxed as an S-corporation, you must file Form 2553 with the IRS within 75 days of incorporation. As a practical matter, you should sign and file this at your incorporation meeting; otherwise, you may forget. Form 2553 is included in this book as Form L, and a filled-in sample is shown in Appendix B. To make the S-corporation status "official" you should also adopt a corporate resolution electing to be taxed as an S-corporation and keep it in your minute book.

Form AP157 (State Sales Tax Application)

If you will be selling or renting goods or services at retail, you must collect Texas Sales and Use Tax. Some services such as doctors' and lawyers' fees are not taxed, but most others are. If you have any doubt, check with the Comptroller of Public Accounts. First, you must obtain a tax number which requires you to fill out a simple questionnaire. To obtain this form you can call the Comptroller (your local office should be listed in the beginning of your phone book under Texas State Government Offices/Comptroller of Public Accounts) or you can write to the Comptroller of Public Accounts, State of Texas, Austin, TX 78774. This form is also included in our book *How to Start a Business in Texas*. After you obtain your tax number, you will be required to collect sales tax on all purchases. Tax returns must be filed quarterly. After a year, if your taxes are low, you may be allowed to file only annually.

Corporate Supplies

Corporate Kits

A corporation needs to keep a permanent record of its legal affairs. This includes the original charter (articles of incorporation and bylaws); minutes of all meetings; records of the stock issued, transferred and cancelled; assumed names registered; and any other legal matters. The records are usually kept in a ring binder. Any ring binder will do, but it is possible to purchase a specially prepared "corporate kit" which has the name of the corporation printed on it and usually contains forms such as minutes, stock certificates, etc. Most of these items are included with this book, so purchasing such a kit is unnecessary unless you want to have a fancy leather binder or specially printed stock certificates.

Some sources for corporate kits are:

Excelsior-Legal, Inc.
610 Magic Mile
P.O. Box 5683
Arlington, TX 76005
(800) 221-2972

Texas Corporation Supplies, Inc.
P.O. Box 12695
Houston, TX 77217
(713) 946-0141
(800) 392-3720

Corpex
480 Canal Street
New York, NY 10013
(800) 221-8181

Corporate Seal

One thing that is not included with this book is a corporate seal. This must be specially made for each corporation. Most corporations use a metal seal like a notary's seal to emboss the paper. These can be ordered from many office supply companies. In recent years, many have been using rubber stamps for corporate seals. These are cheaper, lighter and easier to read. Rubber stamp seals can also be ordered from office supply stores, printers and specialized rubber stamp companies. The corporate seal should contain the *full, exact name of the corporation*, the word "SEAL" and the year of incorporation. It may be round or rectangular.

Stock Certificates and Offers to Purchase Stock (TBCA art. 2.19)

Texas corporations are no longer required to issue stock certificates to represent shares of ownership. However, as a practical matter it is a good idea to do so. This shows some formality and gives each person tangible evidence of ownership. If you do issue shares, the face of each certificate must show the corporate name; that the corporation was organized under Texas law; the name of the shareholder(s); and the number, class and series of the stock. The certificate must be signed by one or more officers designated by the bylaws or the board of directors.

If there are two or more classes or series of stock, the front or back of the certificate must contain (a) a full statement of all of the designations, preferences, limitations and relative rights of each class or series or (b) a statement that the articles of incorporation contain the designations, preferences, limitations and relative rights of each class or series. The certificate must also state that the corporation will make available such a statement to the certificate holder without charge.

The stock certificates can be fancy, with engraved eagles, or they can be typed or even handwritten. Stock certificate forms are included at the end of this book. They should be completed like the sample on the next page. For professional corporations the following statement should be typed on the certificate: "The transfer of the shares represented by this certificate is restricted by the bylaws of the corporation."

Before any stock is issued, the purchaser should submit an "Offer to Purchase Stock" (Form J). The offer states that it is made pursuant to IRS Code §1244. This section originally allowed greater tax deductions in case the stock became worthless. With the new tax laws no longer differentiating between long- and short-term capital gains this would not make a difference, but if the laws change it may again become important.

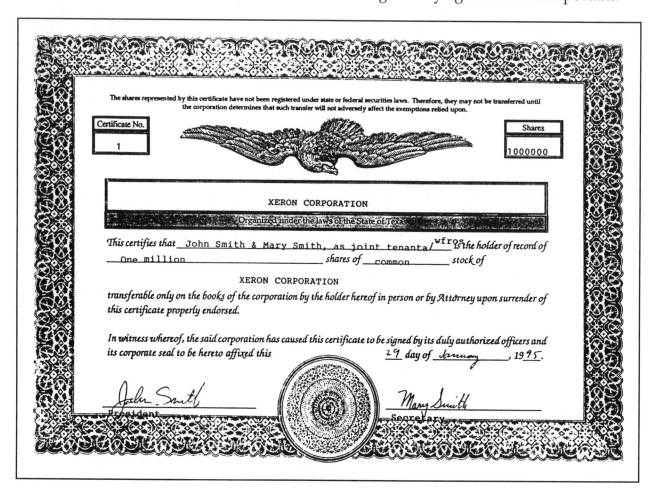

Some thought should be given to the way in which the ownership of the stock will be held. Stock owned in one person's name alone is subject to probate upon death. Making two persons joint owners of the stock (joint tenants with full rights of survivorship) would avoid probate upon the death of one of them. However, taking a joint owner's name off in the event of a disagreement (such as divorce) could be troublesome. Where a couple jointly operates a business, joint ownership would be best. But where one person is the sole party involved in the business the desire to avoid probate should be weighed against the risk of losing half the business in a divorce. Another way to avoid probate is to put ownership of the stock in a living trust. In Texas, stock owned in one spouse's name alone is considered community property and the non-owner spouse is treated as having an ownership interest in one-half of the stock. If the stock is intended to be owned by one spouse alone, the stock certificate should contain language such as "John Doe, as his sole and separate property."

Organizational Meeting

The real birth of the corporation takes place at the initial meeting of the incorporators and the initial board of directors. At this meeting the stock is issued and the officers and board of directors are elected. Other business may also take place, such as electing S-corporation status or adopting employee benefit plans.

Usually minutes, stock certificates, tax and other forms are prepared before the organizational meeting and used as a script for the meeting. They are then signed at the end of the meeting. Otherwise, they may be forgotten until it is too late.

The agenda for the initial meeting is usually as follows:

```
1.   Signing the waiver of notice of the meeting (Form E)
2.   Noting persons present
3.   Presentation and acceptance of articles of incorporation
     (the copy returned by the Secretary of State)
4.   Election of Directors
5.   Adoption of bylaws (Form G or Form H)
6.   Election of officers
7.   Presentation and acceptance of corporate seal
8.   Presentation and acceptance of stock certificate (Form Y)
9.   Designation of bank (Form I)
10.  Resolution accepting stock offers (Form J)
     (Use Form K, Bill of Sale, if property is traded for stock.)
11.  Resolution to pay expenses
12.  Adoption of special resolutions such as S-corporation status
     (Forms L and M)
13.  Adjournment
```

At the end of the meeting the stock certificates are usually issued, but in some cases, such as when a prospective shareholder does not yet have money to pay for them, they are issued when paid for.

To issue the stock, the certificates at the end of this book should be completed by adding the name of the corporation, a statement that the corporation is organized under the laws of Texas, the number of shares the certificate represents and the person to whom the certificate is issued. Each certificate should be numbered in order to keep track of them. A record of the stock issuance should be made on the stock transfer ledger (Form W) and on the "stubs" (Form X). The stubs should be cut apart on the dotted lines, punched and inserted in the ring binder.

Minute Book

After the organizational meeting you should set up your minute book. As noted on page 34, this can be a fancy leather book or a simple ring binder. The minute book usually contains the following:

1. A title page ("Corporate Records of _____")
2. A table of contents
3. The letter from the Secretary of State acknowledging receipt and filing of the articles of incorporation
4. Copy of the articles of incorporation
5. Copy of any assumed name registration
6. Copy of any trademark registration
7. Notice of organizational meeting
8. Minutes of organizational meeting
9. Bylaws
10. Sample stock certificate
11. Offer to purchase stock
12. Tax forms:
    Form SS-4 and Employer Identification Number certificate
    Form 2553 and acceptance
    Form DR-1 and state tax number certificate
13. Stock ledger
14. Stock stubs

Bank Accounts

A corporation must have a bank account. Checks payable to a corporation cannot be cashed; they must be deposited into an account.

Fees

Unfortunately, many banks charge ridiculous rates to corporations for the right to put their money in the bank. You can tell how much extra a corporation is being charged when you compare a corporate account to a personal account with similar activity.

Example:

For similar balance and activity, an individual might earn $6.00 interest for the month while a corporation pays $40.00 in bank fees. Surely the bank is not losing money on every personal account. Therefore, the corporate account is simply generating $40.00 more in profit for the bank. This money will probably be used to buy more art objects or corporate jets for the bank's officers.

Usually, there is a complicated scheme of fees with charges for each transaction. Many banks today are even bold enough to charge companies for the right to make a deposit! (Twenty-five cents for the deposit plus 10¢ for each check which is deposited. Deposit thirty checks and this will cost you $3.25!) Often the customer is granted an interest credit on the balance in the account, but it is usually small and if the credit is larger than the charges, you lose the excess. In some banks the officers cannot even tell you how the fees are figured because the system is so complicated.

Fortunately, some banks have set up reasonable fees for small corporations such as charging no fees if a balance of $1000 or $2500 is maintained. Because the fees can easily amount to hundreds of dollars a year, it pays to shop around. Even if the bank is relatively far from the business, using bank-by-mail can make the distance meaningless. But don't be surprised if a bank with low fees raises them.

As the banking industry got deeper into trouble, fewer and fewer banks were offering reasonable fees for corporate checking accounts. Even with their balance sheets improving, they are not eager to give up this new source of wealth. But you can usually find loopholes if you use your imagination. One trick is to open a checking account and a money market account. (Money market accounts pay higher interest and do not charge for making deposits. You can only write three checks a month but you can usually make unlimited withdrawals.) Then make all of your deposits into the money market account and just pay bills out of the regular checking account, transferring funds as needed. But banks are catching on to this and starting to charge for deposits into money market accounts. So start one at a brokerage firm.

Another way to save money in bank charges is to order checks from a private source rather than through the bank. These are usually much cheaper than those the bank offers because the bank makes a profit on the check printing. If the bank officer doesn't like the idea when you are opening the account, just wait until your first batch runs out and switch over without telling the bank. They probably won't even notice, as long as you get the checks printed correctly. While most "business checks" are large (and expensive), there is no reason you cannot use small "personal size" checks for your business. They are easier to carry around and work just as well unless you want to impress people with the size of your check.

Paperwork

All you should need to open a corporate bank account is a copy of your articles of incorporation and your federal tax identification number. Some banks, however, want more, and they sometimes don't even know what more it is they want. If you have trouble opening the account, you can use the "Banking Resolution" included with this book (Form I), or you can make up a similar form.

Chapter 5

Selling Corporate Stock

Securities Laws

Every issuance of "securities" is subject to both federal and state securities laws. The law is so broad that any instrument which represents an investment in an enterprise, where the investor is relying on the efforts of others, is considered a security. Even a promissory note has been held to be a security. Once an investment is determined to involve a security, all kinds of strict, horrible rules apply. There are criminal penalties, and triple damages can be awarded to "victims." The reason is to protect people who put up money as an investment in a business. In the stock market crash of the early 1930s, many people lost their life savings in swindles, and the government wants to be sure that it won't happen again. Unfortunately, the laws make it nearly impossible to raise capital for many honest businesses.

The basic requirement for issuing securities is that investors be given full disclosure of the risks involved in an investment. To accomplish this, the laws usually require that the securities be registered with the federal Securities and Exchange Commission and/or the State Securities Board, and lengthy disclosure statements compiled and distributed to potential investors.

The law is so complicated and strict, and the penalties so harsh, that most lawyers won't handle securities matters. Those that do have a hard time getting malpractice coverage and often the policies have a $10,000 deductible. So there is not much likelihood that you will be able to get through the registration process on your own. But, like your decision to incorporate without a lawyer, you may want to do a cost/value analysis in this situation. If a lawyer needs to charge at least $20,000 for a securities issuance and you only plan to borrow $50,000 from some friends or relatives, you will probably decide that it is not worth it. After paying a decent return to the investors the net cost of the money may be 50% of what you raise. So you may wish to consider some alternatives:

1.   Take the money as a personal loan from the friends or relatives. The disadvantage is that you will have to pay them back personally if the business fails. However, you may have to do that anyway if the investors are close relatives or if you don't follow the securities laws.

2.   Tailor your stock issuance to fall within the exemptions in the securities laws. Luckily there are some exemptions for small businesses in the securities laws. If you fall into these exemptions the securities laws do not apply to your transaction. The exemptions are explained below, but you should make at least one appointment with a securities lawyer to be sure you have covered everything and that there have not been any changes in the law. Often you can pay for an hour or so of a securities lawyer's time for $100 or $150 and just ask questions about the different plans you have. He or she can tell you what not to do and what your options are, and you then can make an informed decision.

3.   Research the securities laws and do the issuance yourself. This is dangerous since there are criminal penalties for violations and victims are allowed triple damages. However, you may wish to do a cost/value/risk analysis. Who are the investors? Would they sue you? Do you have assets you could liquidate to pay off the investors? Would the legal fees be worth the "insurance" they would provide?

Exemptions From Securities Laws

In situations where one person, or a husband and wife, or a few partners run a business, and all parties are active in the enterprise, securities laws do not apply to their issuance of stock to themselves. These are the simple corporations which are the subject of this book. As a practical matter, if your father or aunt wants to put up some money for some stock in your business, you probably won't get in trouble. They probably won't seek triple damages and criminal penalties if your business fails. (This can't be said of your father-in-law in the event he becomes your ex-father-in-law some day!)

There are other situations which may also be exempt. The following is a brief summary of the possible exemptions:

Federal Exemptions

In recent years the Securities and Exchange Commission (SEC) has greatly simplified the requirements for small businesses that wish to raise capital. The current exemptions are as follows:

Rule 504 Exemption under Regulation D. This exemption applies to all offerings of less than $1 million within a 12-month period. With the recent changes in this rule there are no longer restrictions on how investors are solicited, the number of investors involved, the sophistication of the investor, or the time that the securities must be held. The rule does prohibit the use of this exemption for blind pools (companies with no business plan except to look for opportunities), companies registered under the Investment Company Act of 1940, or companies subject to Securities Exchange Act §12 reporting requirements. Form D must be filed with the SEC within 15 days of the first sale of securities.

In using this exemption, issuers of stock must also comply with the anti-fraud provisions of SEC Rule 10b-5. This rule requires that material facts regarding the investment, including all risks, must be disclosed to purchasers.

Unfortunately, the simplification of federal requirements has not been accompanied by similar changes at the state level. Texas and most states still have much stricter requirements for the issuance of securities. There is a movement to change the laws, but for now the only way to avoid the Texas registration procedures is to qualify for the Texas limited offering described below.

Regulation A Exemption. This exemption applies to all offerings of less than $5 million within a 12-month period. To qualify, Form 1-A must be filed with the SEC office in Atlanta and an offering circular must be prepared and given to investors. There are some restrictions on the resale of the securities by the investors.

Texas Limited Offering Exemption

This exemption can apply if all of the following are true:

• There are 35 or fewer purchasers of shares

• No advertising or general solicitation is used to promote the stock

These rules may sound simple on the surface but there are many more rules, regulations and court cases explaining each one in more detail.

Federal Small Offering Registration

For companies that need to raise more than $5 million, there is a new "SB-2" public offering option. This applies to companies which have less than $25 million in revenues, have less than $25 million in outstanding securities, are not an investment company, and are not a subsidiary of a firm outside of these limits. For more information call the SEC at (202) 272-7460 or (202) 272-7461 and ask for Regulation SB forms and instructions.

Payment for Shares

When issuing stock it is important that full payment be made by the purchasers. If the shares have a par value and the payment is in cash, the cash must not be less than the par value. A promissory note cannot be used in payment for shares. The shares must not be issued until the payment has been received by the corporation.

Trading Property for Shares

In many cases, organizers of a corporation have property they want to contribute for use in starting up the business. This is often the case where a going business is incorporated. To avoid future problems, the property should be traded at a fair value for the shares. The directors should pass a resolution stating that they agree with the value of the property. When the stock certificate is issued in exchange for the property, a bill of sale should be executed by the owner of the property detailing everything that is being exchanged for the stock. A blank bill of sale is included in this book as Form K.

Taxable Transactions

In cases where property is exchanged for something of value, such as stock, there is often income tax due as if there had been a sale of the property. Fortunately, §351 of the IRS Code allows tax-free exchange of property for stock if the persons receiving the stock for the property or for cash *end up owning* at least 80% of the voting and other stock in the corporation. If more than 20% of the stock is issued in exchange for services instead of property and cash, then the transfers of property will be taxable and treated as a sale for cash.

Trading Services for Shares

In some cases, the founders of a corporation wish to issue stock to one or more persons in exchange for their services to the corporation. It has always been possible to issue shares for services which have previously been performed. In 1990, it became legal to issue shares in exchange for a written promises to perform services in the future.

Chapter 6
Running a Corporation

Day to Day Activities

There are not many differences between running a corporation and any other type of business. The most important point to remember is to keep the corporation separate from your personal affairs. Don't be continuously making loans to yourself from corporate funds and don't commingle funds.

Another important point to remember is to always refer to the corporation as a corporation. *Always* use the designation "Inc." or "Corp." on *everything*. *Always* sign corporate documents with your corporate title. If you don't, you may lose your protection from liability. There have been many cases where a person forgot to put the word "pres." after his name and was held personally liable for a corporate debt!

Corporate Records

Minutes

Texas law (TBCA art. 2.44) requires that a corporation keep a permanent record of "minutes of the proceedings of its shareholders, its board of directors, and each committee of the board of directors."

Accounting Records

Accurate accounting records must be kept by the corporation (TBCA art. 2.44).

Record of Shareholders

The corporation must also keep a record of its shareholders, including the names and addresses and the number, class, and series of shares owned (TBCA art. 2.44 (A)). This can be kept at the registered office, principal place of business, or office of its stock transfer agent (if any). The transfer ledger contained in this book as Form W can be used for this purpose.

Corporate Documents

The corporation must maintain copies of its articles of incorporation and all amendments, bylaws and all amendments, resolutions regarding stock rights, minutes of shareholders' meetings and records of actions taken without a meeting for the last 3 years, written communications to all shareholders for the last 3 years, financial statements furnished to shareholders for the last 3 years, names and addresses of all current directors and officers, and the most recent annual report.

Form of Records

The minutes may be in writing or in "any other form capable of being converted into written form within a reasonable time." This would mean that they could be kept in a computer or possibly on a videotape. However, it is always best to keep at least one written copy. Accidents can easily erase magnetic media.

Examination of Records

Any shareholder of a corporation has the right to examine and copy the corporation's books and records after giving written notice within a reasonable time before the date on which he wishes to inspect and copy them, if he has a good faith reason for a proper purpose and he describes his purpose and the records (if the purpose is related to the records) (TBCA art. 2.44 (B)).

The shareholder may have his attorney or agent examine the records and may receive photocopies of the records (TBCA art. 2.44 (B)). The corporation may charge a reasonable fee for making photocopies. If the records are not in written form, the corporation must convert them to written form. The corporation generally must bear the cost of converting the records.

If the corporation refuses to allow a shareholder to examine the records then the shareholder may get an order from the local court, and in such case, the corporation would have to pay the shareholder' costs and attorney fees (TBCA art. 2.44(C)).

Balance Sheets

Upon written request from a shareholder, the corporation must furnish its annual statements for the last fiscal year showing in reasonable detail its assets, liabilities and results of its operations (TBCA art. 2.44 (E)).

Shareholder Meetings

Each year the corporation must hold an annual meeting of the shareholders. These meetings may be formal, for example held in a restaurant, or they may be informal, for example held in the swimming pool. A sole officer and director can hold them in his mind without reciting all the verbiage or taking a formal vote. But the important thing is that the meetings are held and that minutes are kept. Regular minutes and meetings are evidence that the corporation is legitimate if the issue ever comes up in court. Minute forms for the annual meetings are included with this book. You can use them as master copies to photocopy each year. All that needs to be changed is the date, unless you actually change officers or directors or need to take some other corporate action.

Special Meetings

When important decisions must be made by the shareholders between the annual meetings, the corporation can hold special meetings.

Action Without a Meeting

Under the procedures of TBCA art. 9.10 (A), action may be taken by the shareholders without a formal meeting. However, for a small corporation it is best to use formal meetings in case someone later tries to pierce the corporate veil.

Notice of Meetings

Under Texas law (TBCA art. 2.25), shareholders with voting rights must be notified of the date, time and place of annual and special meetings at least 10 but not more than 60 days prior. No description of the purpose of an annual meeting need be given, but the purpose for a special meeting must be stated in the notice.

A shareholder may waive notice either before or after the meeting if done in writing and included in the minutes. Unless a shareholder objects, attendance at a meeting waives objection to the notice or lack thereof.

Voting

The following rules apply to voting at the shareholders' meeting:

• Unless otherwise provided in the articles of incorporation or bylaws, a quorum consists of a majority of the shares entitled to vote (TBCA art. 2.28A)

- Once a share is represented at a meeting for any purpose it is deemed present for quorum purposes for the rest of the meeting (TBCA art. 2.28(A))

- Holders of a majority of the shares represented may adjourn the meeting (TBCA art. 2.28(B))

- The articles of incorporation may authorize a quorum of less than a majority but it may not be less than one-third (TBCA art. 2.28(A)(2))

Voting for Directors

Unless otherwise provided in the articles of incorporation, directors are elected by a plurality of votes. Shareholders do not have a right to cumulative voting unless provided in the articles.

Board of Directors Meetings

Each year the corporation must hold an annual meeting of the directors. These meetings also may be formal, such as those held in a restaurant, or informal, such as those held in the swimming pool. A sole officer and director can hold them in his mind without reciting all the verbiage or taking a formal vote. But the important thing is that the meetings are held and that minutes are kept. Regular minutes and meetings are evidence that the corporation is legitimate if the issue ever comes up in court. Minute forms for the annual meetings are included with this book. You can use them as master copies to photocopy each year. All that needs to be changed is the date, unless you actually change officers or directors or need to take some other corporate action.

Special Meetings

When important decisions must be made by the board of directors between the annual meetings, the corporation can hold special meetings.

Action Without a Meeting

Under the procedures of TBCA art. 9.10 (B), action may be taken by the directors without a formal meeting. However, for a small corporation it is best to use formal meetings in case someone later tries to pierce the corporate veil.

Notice of Meetings

Under Texas law (TBCA 2.37), regular meetings of the board of directors may be held without notice unless the articles of incorporation or bylaws provide otherwise. Directors must be notified of the time, date and place of special meetings within the timeframe prescribed in the bylaws.

Voting

The following rules apply to voting at the directors' meeting:

• Unless otherwise provided in the articles of incorporation or bylaws, a quorum consists of a majority of the number of directors prescribed in the articles or bylaws

• The articles of incorporation may authorize a quorum of less than a majority but it may not be less than one-third

• If a quorum is present for a vote, a vote by a majority of those present constitutes an act of the board of directors unless otherwise provided in the articles or bylaws

Committees

Unless prohibited by the bylaws the board of directors may designate a committee of its members which can exercise all authority of the board except that it may not:

• approve or recommend actions which by law must be approved by the shareholders
• fill vacancies on the board or committees thereof
• adopt, repeal or amend the bylaws
• propose reacquisition of shares
• recommend a voluntary dissolution of the corporation

Also, meeting rules of committees must comply with the rules for the board itself. Each committee must have at least one member and alternate members may be designated. Setting up a committee does not relieve a member of his duty to act in good faith in the best interests of the corporation.

Annual Reports

Each year every corporation must file an annual report. Fortunately, this is a simple one-page form which is sent to the corporation by the Secretary of State. It contains such information as the federal tax identification number, and directors' names and addresses, the registered agent's name and the address of the registered office. It must be signed and returned by May 15th.

Chapter 7

Amending a Corporation

Articles of Incorporation

Because the articles of incorporation included in this book are so basic, they will rarely have to be amended. The only reasons for amending them would be to change the name or the number of shares of stock, or to add some special clause such as a higher than majority voting requirement for directors as provided in TBCA art. 2.35. If the amendment is made before any shares are issued, it may be done by the directors by filing articles of amendment signed by the directors stating the name of the corporation, the amendment and date adopted, and a statement that it is made before any shares were issued. If the amendment is made after shares have been issued, the articles of amendment must be signed by an officer of the corporation.

The articles of amendment must contain the name of the corporation, the amendments, the date of adoption by the shareholders, the number of shares voting for and against the amendment and, if the change affects the outstanding shares, a statement of how the change will be effected. The articles of amendment must be filed with the Secretary of State along with the filing fee of $150. The procedure for amending corporate articles depends upon who is doing the amending and at what point in time the amendment is adopted. For more information you should refer to TBCA art. 4.01 through 4.07, which is included in Appendix A of this book.

Bylaws

The shareholders may always amend the bylaws. The board of directors may amend the bylaws unless the articles of incorporation state otherwise or unless the shareholders provide that the bylaws may not be amended by the board (TBCA art. 2.23).

Registered Agent or Registered Office

To change the registered agent or registered office, a form must be sent to the Secretary of State with the fee of $15. This form is included in this book as Form V. This form can be used to change both the registered agent and the registered office or to just change one of them. If you are changing just one, such as the agent, then list the registered office as both the old address and the new address.

Chapter 8
Checklist for Forming a Simple Corporation

Checklist for Forming a Simple Corporation

√ Decide on corporate name

√ Prepare and file Articles of Incorporation

√ Send for Federal Employer Identification Number (IRS Form SS-4)

√ Prepare Shareholders' Agreement, if necessary

√ Meet with accountant to discuss capitalization and tax planning

√ If necessary, meet with securities lawyer regarding stock sales

√ Obtain corporate seal and ring binder for minutes

√ Hold organizational meeting

    √ Complete Bylaws, Waiver, Minutes, Offers to Purchase Stock

    √ Sign all documents and place in minute book

√ Issue stock certificates

    √ Be sure consideration is paid

    √Complete Bill of Sale if property is traded for stock

    √ Put documentary stamps on stubs in minute book

√ File Assumed Name if one will be used

√ Open Bank account

√ For S-Corporation status, file Form 2553

Appendix A
Selected Texas Statutes

Art. 1.02. Definitions

A. As used in this Act, unless the context otherwise requires, the term:

(1) "Articles of incorporation" means the original or restated articles of incorporation and all amendments thereto.

(2) "Authorized shares" means the shares of all classes which the corporation is authorized to issue.

(3) "Cancel" means to restore issued shares to the status of authorized but unissued shares.

(4) "Certificated shares" means shares represented by instruments in bearer or registered form.

(5) "Conspicuous" or "conspicuously," when prescribed for information appearing on a certificate for shares or other securities, means the location of such information or use of type of sufficient size, color, or character that a reasonable person against whom such information may operate should notice it. For example, a printed or typed statement in capitals, or bold face or underlined type, or in type that is larger than or that contrasts in color with that used for other statements on the same certificate, is "conspicuous."

(6) "Consuming assets corporation" means a corporation which is engaged in the business of exploiting assets subject to depletion or amortization and which elects to state in its articles of incorporation that it is a consuming assets corporation and includes as a part of its official corporate name the phrase "a consuming assets corporation," giving such phrase equal prominence with the rest of the corporate name on its financial statements and certificates representing shares. All its certificates representing shares shall also contain a further sentence: "This corporation is permitted by law to pay dividends out of reserves which may impair its stated capital."

(7) "Corporation" or "domestic corporation" means a corporation for profit subject to the provisions of this Act, except a foreign corporation.

(8) "Distribution" means a transfer of money or other property (except its own shares or rights to acquire its own shares), or issuance of indebtedness, by a corporation to its shareholders in the form of:

(a) a dividend on any class or series of the corporation's outstanding shares;

(b) a purchase, redemption, or other acquisition by the corporation, directly or indirectly, of any of its own shares; or

(c) a payment by the corporation in liquidation of all or a portion of its assets.

(9) "Foreign corporation" means a corporation for profit organized under laws other than the laws of this State.

(10) "Insolvency" means inability of a corporation to pay its debts as they become due in the usual course of its business.

(11) "Investment Company Act" means the Investment Company Act of 1940 (15 U.S.C. Sec. 80a-1 et seq.);

(12) "Merger" means (a) the division of a domestic corporation into two or more new domestic corporations or into a surviving corporation and one or more new domestic or foreign corporations or other entities, or (b) the combination of one or more domestic corporations with one or more domestic or foreign corporations or other entities resulting in (i) one or more surviving domestic or foreign corporations or other entities, (ii) the creation of one or more new domestic or foreign corporations or other entities, or (iii) one or more surviving domestic or foreign corporations or other entities and the creation of one or more new domestic or foreign corporations or other entities.

(13) "Net assets" means the amount by which the total assets of a corporation exceed the total debts of the corporation.

(14) "Other entity" means any entity, whether organized for profit or not, that is a corporation (other than a domestic or foreign corporation), limited or general partnership, joint venture, joint stock company, cooperative, association, bank, insurance company or other legal entity organized pursuant to the laws of this state or any other state or country to the extent such laws or the constituent documents of that entity, not inconsistent with such laws, permit that entity to enter into a merger or share exchange as permitted by Article 5.03 of this Act.

(15) "Share dividend" means a dividend by a corporation that is payable in its own authorized but unissued shares or in treasury shares.

(16) "Shareholder" or "holder of shares" means the person in whose name shares issued by a corporation are registered at the relevant time in the share transfer records maintained by the corporation pursuant to Article 2.44 of this Act.

(17) "Shares" means the units into which the proprietary interests in a corporation are divided, whether certificated or uncertificated shares.

(18) "Stated capital" means, at any particular time, the sum of:

(a) the par value of all shares of the corporation having a par value that have been issued;

(b) the consideration fixed by the corporation in the manner provided by Article 2.15 of this Act for all shares of the corporation without par value that have been issued, except such part of the consideration that is actually received therefor (which part must be less than all of that consideration) that the board by resolution adopted no later than sixty (60) days after the issuance of those shares may have allocated to surplus; and

(c) such amounts not included in paragraphs (a) and (b) of this subsection as have been transferred to stated capital of the corporation, whether upon the payment of a share dividend or upon adoption by the board of directors of a resolution directing that all or part of surplus be transferred to stated capital, minus all reductions from such sum as have been effected in a manner permitted by law.

(19) "Subscriber" means the offeror in a subscription.

(20) "Subscription" means a memorandum in writing, executed before or after incorporation, wherein an offer is made to purchase and pay for a specified number of theretofore unissued shares of a corporation.

(21) "Surplus" means the excess of the net assets of a corporation over its stated capital.

(22) "Treasury shares" means shares of a corporation which have been issued, have been subsequently acquired by and belong to the corporation, and have not been canceled and restored to the status of authorized but unissued shares. Treasury shares shall be deemed to be "issued" shares but not "outstanding" shares, and shall not be included in the total assets of a corporation for purposes of determining its "net assets."

(23) "Uncertificated shares" means shares not represented by instruments and the transfers of which are registered upon books maintained for that purpose by or on behalf of the issuing corporation.

B. Part Twelve of this Act provides definitions of terms used in the Texas Close Corporation Law.

C. A reference in this Act to another statute is a reference to that statute as amended.

PART TWO

Art. 2.01. Purposes

A. Except as hereinafter in this Article excluded herefrom, corporations for profit may be organized under this Act for any lawful purpose or purposes. Corporations for the purpose of operating non-profit institutions, including but not limited to those devoted to charitable, benevolent, religious, patriotic, civic, cultural, missionary, educational, scientific, social, fraternal, athletic, or aesthetic purposes, may not adopt or be organized under this Act.

B. No corporation may adopt this Act or be organized under this Act or obtain authority to transact business in this State under this Act:

(1) If any one or more of its purposes for the transaction of business in this State is expressly prohibited by any law of this State.

(2) If any one or more of its purposes for the transaction of business in this State is to engage in any activity which cannot lawfully be engaged in without first obtaining a license under the authority of the laws of this State to engage in such activity and such a license cannot lawfully be granted to a corporation.

(3) If among its purposes for the transaction of business in this State, there is included, however worded, a combination of the two businesses listed in either of the following:

(a) The business of raising cattle and owning land therefor, and the business of operating stockyards and of slaughtering, refrigerating, canning, curing or packing

meat. Owning and operating feed lots and feeding cattle shall not be considered as engaging in "the business of raising cattle and owning land therefor" within the purview of this paragraph of this subsection.

(b) The business of engaging in the petroleum oil producing business in this State and the business of engaging directly in the oil pipe line business in this State: provided, however, that a corporation engaged in the oil producing business in this State which owns or operates private pipe lines in and about its refineries, fields or stations or which owns stock of corporations engaged in the oil pipe line business shall not be deemed to be engaging directly in the oil pipe line business in this State; and provided that any corporation, or group of corporations acting in partnership or other combination with other corporations, engaged as a common carrier in the pipe line business for transporting oil, oil products, gas, carbon dioxide, salt brine, fuller's earth, sand, clay, liquefied minerals or other mineral solutions, shall have all of the rights and powers conferred by Sections 111.019 through 111.022, Natural Resources Code.

(4) If any one or more of its purposes is to operate any of the following:

(a) Banks, (b) trust companies, (c) building and loan associations or companies, (d) insurance companies of every type and character that operate under the insurance laws of this State, and corporate attorneys in fact for reciprocal or inter-insurance exchanges, (e) railroad companies, (f) cemetery companies, (g) cooperatives or limited cooperative associations, (h) labor unions, (i) abstract and title insurance companies whose purposes are provided for and whose powers are prescribed by Chapter 9 of the Insurance Code of this State.

C. A company may be incorporated under this Article or under Chapter 1, Title 112, Revised Statutes, if the company:

(1) operates a railroad passenger service by contracting with a railroad corporation or other company; and

(2) does not construct, own, or maintain a railroad track.

Art. 2.02. General Powers

A. Subject to the provisions of Sections B and C of this Article, each corporation shall have power:

(1) To have perpetual succession by its corporate name unless a limited period of duration is stated in its articles of incorporation. Notwithstanding the articles of incorporation, the period of duration for any corporation incorporated before September 6, 1955, is perpetual if all fees and franchise taxes have been paid as provided by law.

(2) To sue and be sued, complain and defend, in its corporate name.

(3) To have a corporate seal which may be altered at pleasure, and to use the same by causing it, or a facsimile thereof, to be impressed on, affixed to, or in any manner reproduced upon, instruments of any nature required to be executed by its proper officers.

(4) To purchase, receive, lease, or otherwise acquire, own, hold, improve, use and otherwise deal in and with, real or personal property, or any interest therein, wherever situated, as the purposes of the corporation shall require.

(5) To sell, convey, mortgage, pledge, lease, exchange, transfer and otherwise dispose of all or any part of its property and assets.

(6) To lend money to, and otherwise assist, its employees, officers, and directors if such a loan or assistance reasonably may be expected to benefit, directly or indirectly, the lending or assisting corporation.

(7) To purchase, receive, subscribe for, or otherwise acquire, own, hold, vote, use, employ, mortgage, lend, pledge, sell or otherwise dispose of, and otherwise use and deal in and with, shares or other interests in, or obligations of, other domestic or foreign corporations, associations, partnerships, or individuals, or direct or indirect obligations of the United States or of any other government, state, territory, government district, or municipality, or of any instrumentality thereof.

(8) To purchase or otherwise acquire its own bonds, debentures, or other evidences of its indebtedness or obligations; to purchase or otherwise acquire its own unredeemable shares and hold those acquired shares as treasury shares or cancel or otherwise dispose of those acquired shares; and to redeem or purchase shares made redeemable by the provisions of its articles of incorporation.

(9) To make contracts and incur liabilities, borrow money at such rates of interest as the corporation may determine, issue its notes, bonds, and other obligations, and secure any of its obligations by mortgage or pledge of all or any of its property, franchises, and income.

(10) To lend money for its corporate purposes, invest and reinvest its funds, and take and hold real and personal property as security for the payment of funds so loaned or invested.

(11) To conduct its business, carry on its operations, and have offices and exercise the powers granted by this Act, within or without this State.

(12) To elect or appoint officers and agents of the corporation for such period of time as the corporation may determine, and define their duties and fix their compensation.

(13) To make and alter bylaws, not inconsistent with its articles of incorporation or with the laws of this State, for the administration and regulation of the affairs of the corporation.

(14) To make donations for the public welfare or for charitable, scientific, or educational purposes.

(15) To transact any lawful business which the board of directors shall find will be in aid of government policy.

(16) To indemnify directors, officers, employees, and agents of the corporation and to purchase and maintain liability insurance for those persons.

(17) To pay pensions and establish pension plans, pension trusts, profit sharing plans, stock bonus plans, and other incentive plans for any or all of, or any class or classes of, its directors, officers, or employees.

(18) To be an organizer, partner, member, associate, or manager of any partnership, joint venture, or other enterprise, and to the extent permitted in any other jurisdiction to be an incorporator of any other corporation of any type or kind.

(19) To cease its corporate activities and terminate its existence by voluntary dissolution.

(20) Whether included in the foregoing or not, to have and exercise all powers necessary or appropriate to effect any or all of the purposes for which the corporation is organized.

B. Nothing in this Article grants any authority to officers or directors of a corporation for the exercise of any of the foregoing powers, inconsistent with limitations on any of the same which may be expressly set forth in this Act or in the articles of incorporation or in any other laws of this State. Authority of officers and directors to act beyond the scope of the purpose or purposes of a corporation is not granted by any provision of this Article.

C. Nothing contained in this Article shall be deemed to authorize any action in violation of the Anti-Trust Laws of this State, as now existing or hereafter amended.

Art. 2.02-1. Power to Indemnify and to Purchase Indemnity Insurance; Duty to Indemnify

A. In this article:

(1) "Corporation" includes any domestic or foreign predecessor entity of the corporation in a merger, consolidation, or other transaction in which the liabilities of the predecessor are transferred to the corporation by operation of law and in any other transaction in which the corporation assumes the liabilities of the predecessor but does not specifically exclude liabilities that are the subject matter of this article.

(2) "Director" means any person who is or was a director of the corporation and any person who, while a director of the corporation, is or was serving at the request of the corporation as a director, officer, partner, venturer, proprietor, trustee, employee, agent, or similar functionary of another foreign or domestic corporation, partnership, joint venture, sole proprietorship, trust, employee benefit plan, or other enterprise.

(3) "Expenses" include court costs and attorneys' fees.

(4) "Official capacity" means

(a) when used with respect to a director, the office of director in the corporation, and

(b) when used with respect to a person other than a director, the elective or appointive office in the corporation held by the officer or the employment or agency relationship undertaken by the employee or agent in behalf of the corporation, but

(c) in both Paragraphs (a) and (b) does not include service for any other foreign or domestic corporation or any partnership, joint venture, sole proprietorship, trust, employee benefit plan, or other enterprise.

(5) "Proceeding" means any threatened, pending, or completed action, suit, or proceeding, whether civil, criminal, administrative, arbitrative, or investigative, any appeal in such an action, suit, or proceeding, and any inquiry or investigation that could lead to such an action, suit, or proceeding.

B. A corporation may indemnify a person who was, is, or is threatened to be made a named defendant or respondent in a proceeding because the person is or was a director only if it is determined in accordance with Section F of this article that the person:

(1) conducted himself in good faith;

(2) reasonably believed:

(a) in the case of conduct in his official capacity as a director of the corporation, that his conduct was in the corporation's best interests; and

(b) in all other cases, that his conduct was at least not opposed to the corporation's best interests; and

(b) when used with respect to a person other than a director, the elective or appointive office in the corporation held by an officer or the employment or agency relationship undertaken by the employee or agent in behalf of the corporation, but

(c) in both Paragraphs (a) and (b) does not include service for any other foreign or domestic corporation or any partnership, joint venture, sole proprietorship, trust, employee benefit plan, or other enterprise.

(5) "Proceeding" means any threatened, pending, or completed action, suit, or proceeding, whether civil, criminal, administrative, arbitrative, or investigative, any appeal in such an action, suit, or proceeding, and any inquiry or investigation that could lead to such an action, suit, or proceeding.

B. A corporation may indemnify a person who was, is, or is threatened to be made a named defendant or respondent in a proceeding because the person is or was a director only if it determined in accordance with Section F of this article that the person:

(1) conducted himself in good faith;

(2) reasonably believed:

(a) in the case of conduct in his official capacity as a director of the corporation, that his conduct was in the corporation's best interests; and

(b) in all other cases, that his conduct was at least not opposed to the corporation's best interests; and

(3) in the case of any criminal proceeding, had no reasonable cause to believe his conduct was unlawful.

C. Except to the extent permitted by Section E of this article, a director may not be indemnified under Section B of this article in respect of a proceeding.

(1) in which the person is found liable on the basis that personal benefit was improperly received by him, whether or not the benefit resulted from an action taken in the person's official capacity; or

(2) in which the person is found liable to the corporation.

D. The termination of a proceeding by judgment, order, settlement, or conviction, or on a plea of nolo contendere or its equivalent is not of itself determinative that the person did not meet the requirements set forth in Section B of this article. A person shall be deemed to have been found liable in respect of any claim, issue or matter only after the person shall have been so adjudged by a court of competent jurisdiction after exhaustion of all appeals therefrom.

E. A person may be indemnified under Section B of this article against judgments, penalties (including excise and similar taxes), fines, settlements, and reasonable expenses actually incurred by the person in connection with the proceeding; but if the person is found liable to the corporation or is found liable on the basis that personal benefit was improperly received by the person, the indemnification (1) is limited to reasonable expenses actually incurred by the person in connection with the proceeding and (2) shall not be made in respect of any proceeding in which the person shall have been found liable for willful or intentional misconduct in the performance of his duty to the corporation.

F. A determination of indemnification under Section B of this article must be made:

(1) by a majority vote of a quorum consisting of directors who at the time of the vote are not named defendants or respondents in the proceeding;

(2) if such a quorum cannot be obtained, by a majority vote of a committee of the board of directors, designated to act in the matter by a majority vote of all directors, consisting solely of two or more directors who at the time of the vote are not named defendants or respondents in the proceeding;

(3) by special legal counsel selected by the board of directors or a committee of the board by vote as set forth in Subsection (1) or (2) of this section, or, if such a quorum cannot be obtained and such a committee cannot be established, by a majority vote of all directors; or

(4) by the shareholders in a vote that excludes the shares held by directors who are named defendants or respondents in the proceeding.

G. Authorization of indemnification and determination as to reasonableness of expenses must be made in the same manner as the determination that indemnification is permissible, except that if the determination that indemnification is permissible is made by special legal counsel, authorization of indemnification and determination as to reasonableness of expenses must be made in the manner specified by Subsection (3) of Section F of this article for the selection of special legal counsel. A provision contained in the articles of incorporation, the bylaws, a resolution of shareholders or directors, or an agreement that makes mandatory the indemnification permitted under Section B of this article shall be deemed to constitute authorization of in the manner required by this section even though such provision may not have been adopted or authorized in the same manner as the determination that indemnification is permissible.

H. A corporation shall indemnify a director against reasonable expenses incurred by him in connection with a proceeding in which he is a named defendant or respondent because he is or was a director if he has been wholly successful, on the merits or otherwise, in the defense of the proceeding.

I. If, in a suit for the indemnification required by Section H of this article, a court of competent jurisdiction determines that the director is entitled to indemnification under that section, the court shall order indemnification and shall award to the director the expenses incurred in securing the indemnification.

J. If, upon application of a director, a court of competent jurisdiction determines, after giving any notice the court considers necessary, that the director is fairly and reasonably entitled to indemnification in view of all the relevant circumstances, whether or not he has met the requirements set forth in Section B of this article or has been found liable in the circumstances described by Section C of this article, the court may order the indemnification that the court determines is proper and equitable; but if the person is found liable to the corporation or is found liable on the basis that personal benefit was improperly received by the person, the indemnification shall be limited to reasonable expenses actually incurred by the person in connection with the proceeding.

K. Reasonable expenses incurred by a director who was, is, or is threatened to be made a named defendant or respondent in a proceeding may be paid or reimbursed by the corporation, in advance of the final disposition of the proceeding and without the determination specified in Section F of this article or the authorization or determination specified in Section G of this article, after the corporation receives a written affirmation by the director of his good faith belief that he has met the standard of conduct necessary for indemnification under this article and a written undertaking by or on behalf of the director to repay the amount paid or reimbursed if it is ultimately determined that he has not met that standard or if it is ultimately determined that indemnification of the director against expenses incurred by him in connection with that proceeding is prohibited by Section E of this article. A provision contained in the articles of incorporation, the bylaws, a resolution of shareholders or directors, or an agreement that makes mandatory the payment or reimbursement permitted under this section shall be deemed to constitute authorization of that payment or reimbursement.

L. The written undertaking required by Section K of this article must be an unlimited general obligation of the director but need not be secured. It may be accepted without reference to financial ability to make repayment.

M. A provision for a corporation to indemnify or to advance expenses to a director who was, is, or is threatened to be made a named defendant or respondent in a proceeding, whether contained in the articles of incorporation, the bylaws, a resolution of shareholders or directors, an agreement, or otherwise, except in accordance with Section R of this article, is valid only to the extent it is consistent with this article as limited by the articles of incorporation, if such a limitation exists.

N. Notwithstanding any other provision of this article, a corporation may pay or reimburse expenses incurred by a director in connection with his appearance as a witness or other participation in a proceeding at a time when he is not a named defendant or respondent in the proceeding.

O. An officer of the corporation shall be indemnified as, and to the same extent, provided by Sections H, I, and J of this article for a director and is entitled to seek indemnification under those sections to the same extent as a director. A corporation may indemnify and advance expenses to an officer, employee, or agent of the corporation to the same extent that it may indemnify and advance expenses to directors under this article.

P. A corporation may indemnify and advance expenses to persons who are not or were not officers. employees, or agents of the corporation but who are or were serving at the request of the corporation as a director, officer, partner, venturer, proprietor, trustee, employee, agent, or similar functionary of another foreign or domestic corporation, partnership, joint venture, sole proprietor-

ship, trust, employee benefit plan, or other enterprise to the same extent that it may indemnify and advance expenses to directors under this article.

Q. A corporation may indemnify and advance expenses to an officer, employee, agent, or person identified in Section P of this article and who is not a director to such further extent, consistent with law, as may be provided by its articles of incorporation, bylaws, general or specific action of its board of directors, or contract or as permitted or required by common law.

R. A corporation may purchase and maintain insurance or another arrangement on behalf of any person who is or was a director, officer, employee, or agent of the corporation or who is or was serving at the request of the corporation as a director, officer, partner, venture, proprietor, trustee, employee, agent, or similar functionary of another foreign or domestic corporation, partnership, joint venture, sole proprietorship, trust, employee benefit plan, or other enterprise, against any liability asserted against him and incurred by him in such a capacity or arising out of his status as such a person, whether or not the corporation would have the power to indemnify him against that liability under this article. If the insurance or other arrangement is with a person or entity that is not regularly engaged in the business of providing insurance coverage, the insurance or arrangement may provide for payment of a liability with respect to which the corporation would not have the power to indemnify the person only if including coverage for the additional liability has been approved by the shareholders of the corporation. Without limiting the power of the corporation to procure or maintain any kind of insurance or other arrangement, a corporation may, for the benefit of persons indemnified by the corporation, (1) create a trust fund; (2) establish any form of self-insurance; (3) secure its indemnity obligation by grant of a security interest or other lien on the assets of the corporation; or (4) establish a letter of credit, guaranty, or surety arrangement. The insurance or other arrangement may be procured, maintained, or established within the corporation or with any insurer or other person deemed appropriate by the board of directors regardless of whether all or part of the stock or other securities of the insurer or other person are owned in whole or part by the corporation. In the absence of fraud, the judgment of the board of directors as to the terms and conditions of the insurance or other arrangement and the identity of the insurer or other person participating in an arrangement shall be conclusive and the insurance or arrangement shall not be voidable and shall not subject the directors approving the insurance or arrangement to liability, on any ground, regardless of whether directors participating in the approval are beneficiaries of the insurance or arrangement.

S. Any indemnification of or advance of expenses to a director in accordance with this article shall be reported in writing to the shareholders with or before the notice or waiver of notice of the next shareholders' meeting or with or before the next submission to shareholders of a consent to action without a meeting pursuant to Section A, Article 9.10, of this Act and, in any case, within the

12-month period immediately following the date of the indemnification or advance.

T. For purposes of this article, the corporation is deemed to have requested a director to serve an employee benefit plan whenever the performance by him of his duties to the corporation also imposes duties on or otherwise involves services by him to the plan or participants or beneficiaries of the plan. Excise taxes assessed on a director with respect to an employee benefit plan pursuant to applicable law are deemed fines. Action taken or omitted by him with respect to an employee benefit plan in the performance of his duties for a purpose reasonably believed by him to be in the interest of the participants and beneficiaries of the plan is deemed to be for a purpose which is not opposed to the best interests of the corporation.

U. The articles of incorporation of a corporation may restrict the circumstances under which the corporation is required or permitted to indemnify a person under Section H, I, J, O, P, or Q of this article.

Art. 2.04. Defense of Ultra Vires

A. Lack of capacity of a corporation shall never be made the basis of any claim or defense at law or in equity.

B. No act of a corporation and no conveyance or transfer of real or personal property to or by a corporation shall be invalid by reason of the fact that such act, conveyance or transfer was beyond the scope of the purpose or purposes of the corporation as expressed in its articles of incorporation or by reason of limitations on authority of its officers and directors to exercise any statutory power of the corporation, as such limitations are expressed in the articles of incorporation, but that such act, conveyance or transfer was, or is, beyond the scope of the purpose or purposes of the corporation as expressed in its articles of incorporation or inconsistent with any such expressed limitations of authority, may be asserted:

(1) In a proceeding by a shareholder against the corporation to enjoin the doing of any act or acts or the transfer of real or personal property by or to the corporation. If the unauthorized act or transfer sought to be enjoined is being, or is to be, performed or made pursuant to any contract to which the corporation is a party, the court may, if all of the parties to the contract are parties to the proceeding and if it deems the same to be equitable, set aside and enjoin the performance of such contract, and in so doing may allow to the corporation or to the other parties to the contract, as the case may be, compensation for the loss or damage sustained by either of them which may result from the action of the court in setting aside and enjoining the performance of such contract, but anticipated profits to be derived from the performance of the contract shall not be awarded by the court as a part of loss or damage sustained.

(2) In a proceeding by the corporation, whether acting directly or through a receiver, trustee, or other legal representative, or through shareholders in a representative suit, against the incumbent or former officers or directors of the corporation for exceeding their authority.

(3) In a proceeding by the Attorney General, as provided in this Act, to dissolve the corporation, or in a proceeding by the Attorney General to enjoin the corporation from transacting unauthorized business, or to enforce divestment of real property acquired or held contrary to the laws of this State.

Art. 2.05. Corporate Name; Use of Assumed Names

A. The Corporate name shall conform to the following requirements:

(1) It shall contain the word "corporation," "company," or "incorporated," or shall contain an abbreviation of one of such words, and shall contain such additional words as may be required by law.

(2) It shall not contain any word or phrase which indicates or implies that it is organized for any purpose other than one or more of the purposes contained in its articles of incorporation.

(3) It shall not be the same as, or deceptively similar to, the name of any domestic corporation existing under the laws of this State, or the name of any foreign corporation authorized to transact business in this State, or a name the exclusive right to which is, at the time, reserved in the manner provided in this Act, or the name of a corporation which has in effect a registration of its corporate name as provided in this Act; provided that a name may be similar if written consent is obtained from the existing corporation having the name deemed to be similar or the person, or corporation, for whom the name deemed to be similar is reserved in the office of the Secretary of State.

(4) It shall not contain the word "lottery."

B. Any domestic or foreign corporation having authority to transact business in this State may do so under an assumed name by filing an assumed name certificate in the manner prescribed by law. The assumed name may, but is not required to, comply with the requirements of Section A(1) of this Article.

C. The filing of articles of incorporation under Part Three of this Act, an application to reserve a specified Corporate name under Article 2.06 of this Act, or an application to register a Corporate name by a foreign corporation under Article 2.07 of this Act does not authorize the use of a Corporate name in this State in violation of the rights of another under the federal Trademark Act of 1946 (15 U.S.C., Section 1051 et seq.), the Texas trademark law (Chapter 16, Business & Commerce Code), the Assumed Business or Professional Name Act (Chapter 36, Business & Commerce Code), or the common law. The Secretary of State shall deliver to each newly organized corporation, applicant for reservation of a Corporate name, and newly registered foreign corporation a notice containing the substance of this section.

Art. 2.06. Reserved Name

A. The exclusive right to the use of a corporate name may be reserved by:

(1) Any person intending to organize a corporation under this Act.

(2) Any domestic corporation intending to change its name.

(3) Any foreign corporation intending to make application for a certificate of authority to transact business in this State.

(4) Any foreign corporation authorized to transact business in this State and intending to change its name.

(5) Any person intending to organize a foreign corporation and intending to have such corporation make application for a certificate of authority to transact business in this State.

B. The reservation shall be made by filing with the Secretary of State an application to reserve a specified corporate name, executed by the applicant or the attorney or agent thereof. If the Secretary of State finds that the name is available for corporate use, he shall reserve the same for the exclusive use of the applicant for a period of one hundred and twenty(120) days.

C. The right to the exclusive use of a specified corporate name so reserved may be transferred to any other person or corporation by filing in the office of the Secretary of State a notice of such transfer, executed by the applicant for whom the name was reserved, and specifying the name and address of the transferee.

Art. 2.07. Registered Name

A. Any corporation organized for the purpose of operating a bank, trust company, building and loan association or company, insurance company currently holding a valid certificate of authority to do business in the State of Texas, and any foreign corporation not authorized to transact business in this State may register its corporate name under this Act, provided its corporate name is not the same as, or deceptively similar to, the name of any domestic corporation existing under the laws of this State or the name of any foreign corporation authorized to transact business in this State or any corporate name reserved or registered under this Act. Provided, however, that any bank, trust company, building and loan association, or insurance company will not be prohibited from registering its corporate name even if the corporate name may be deemed to be the same as or deceptively similar to an otherwise authorized corporate name, if such bank, trust company, building and loan association, or insurance company was duly organized on, and in continual existence from, a date preceding the date the conflicting corporate name was authorized by the Secretary of State under this Act.

B. Such registration shall be made by:

(1) Filing with the Secretary of State:

(a) An application for registration executed by the corporation by an officer thereof, setting forth the name of the corporation, the state or territory under the laws of which it is incorporated, the date of its incorporation, a statement that it is carrying on or doing business, and a brief statement of the business in which it is engaged, and

(b) A certificate setting forth that such corporation is in good standing under the laws of the state or territory wherein it is organized, executed by the Secretary of State of such state or territory or by such other official as may have custody of the records pertaining to corpora-

tions, and (2) Paying to the Secretary of State the required registration fee.

C. Such registration shall be effective for a period of one year from the date on which the application for registration is filed, unless voluntarily withdrawn by the filing of a written notice thereof with the Secretary of State.

Art. 2.08. Renewal of Registered Name

A. A corporation which has in effect a registration of its corporate name may renew such registration from year to year by filing annually an application for renewal in the manner prescribed for the filing of an original application. Such renewal application shall be filed during the ninety (90) days preceding the expiration date of the then current registration.

Art. 2.09. Registered Office and Registered Agent

A. Each corporation shall have and continuously maintain in this State:

(1) A registered office which may be, but need not be, the same as its place of business.

(2) A registered agent, which agent may be either an individual resident in this State whose business office is identical with such registered office, or a domestic corporation, or a foreign corporation authorized to transact business in this State which has a business office identical with such registered office.

* * *

Art. 2.11. Service of Process on Corporation

A. The president and all vice presidents of the corporation and the registered agent of the corporation shall be agents of such corporation upon whom any process, notice, or demand required or permitted by law to be served upon the corporation may be served.

B. Whenever a corporation shall fail to appoint or maintain a registered agent in this State, or whenever its registered agent cannot with reasonable diligence be found at the registered office, then the Secretary of State shall be an agent of such corporation upon whom any such process, notice, or demand may be served. Service on the Secretary of State of any process, notice, or demand shall be made by delivering to and leaving with him, or with the Assistant Secretary of State, or with any clerk having charge of the corporation department of his office, duplicate copies of such process, notice, or demand. In the event any such process, notice, or demand is served on the Secretary of State, he shall immediately cause one of the copies thereof to be forwarded by registered mail, addressed to the corporation at its registered office. Any service so had on the Secretary of State shall be returnable in not less than thirty (30) days.

C. The Secretary of State shall keep a record of all processes, notices and demands served upon him under this Article, and shall record therein the time of such service and his action with reference thereto.

Art. 2.12. Authorized Shares

A. Each corporation may issue the number of shares stated in its articles of incorporation. Such shares may be divided into one or more classes, any or all of which classes may consist of shares with par value or shares without par value, as shall be stated in the articles of incorporation. Any such class of shares may be divided into one or more series, as shall be stated in the articles of incorporation. All shares of the same class shall be of the same par value or be without par value. Unless the shares of a class have been divided into series, all shares of the same class may vary between series, but all shares of the same series shall be identical in all respects. Any such class or series of shares shall be so designated as to distinguish the shares of that class or series from the shares of all other classes and series. Any such class or series shall have such designations, preferences, limitations, and relative rights, including voting rights, as shall be stated in the articles of incorporation. The articles of incorporation may limit or deny the voting rights of, or provide special voting rights for, the shares of any class or series to the extent that such limitation, denial, or provision is not inconsistent with the provisions of this Act. Any of the designations, preferences, limitations, and relative rights, including voting rights, of any class or series of shares may be made dependent upon facts ascertainable outside the articles of incorporation, which facts may include future acts of the corporation, provided that the manner in which such facts shall operate upon the designations, preferences, limitations, and relative rights, including voting rights, of such class or series of shares is clearly and expressly set forth in the articles of incorporation.

B. Without being limited to the authority herein contained, a corporation, when so provided in its articles of incorporation, may issue shares of one or more classes or series:

(1) Redeemable, subject to compliance by the corporation with Articles 2.38 and 4.08 of this Act, at the option of the corporation, the shareholder or another person or upon the occurrence of a designated event.

(2) Entitling the holders thereof to cumulative, non-cumulative, or partially cumulative dividends.

(3) Having preference over any other class, classes or series of shares as to the payment of dividends.

(4) Having preference in the assets of the corporation over any other class, classes or series of shares upon the voluntary or involuntary liquidation of the corporation.

(5) Exchangeable, subject to compliance by the corporation with Article 2.38 of this Act, at the option of the corporation, the shareholder or another person or upon the occurrence of a designated event, for shares, obligations, indebtedness, evidence of ownership, rights to purchase securities or other securities of the corporation or one or more other domestic or foreign corporations or other entities or for other property or for any combination of the foregoing.

(6) Convertible at the option of the corporation, the shareholder or another person or upon the occurrence of a designated event, into shares of any other class or series, but shares without par value shall not be converted into shares with par value unless that part of the stated capital of the corporation represented by such shares without par value is, at the time of conversion, at least equal to the aggregate par value of the shares into which shares without par value are to be converted or the amount of any such deficiency is transferred from surplus to stated capital.

C. (1) The board of directors of a corporation registered as an open-end company under the Investment Company Act may:

(a) establish classes of shares and series of unissued shares of any class by fixing and determining the designations, preferences, limitations, and relative rights, including voting rights, of the shares of any class or series so established to the same extent that the designations, preferences, limitations, and relative rights could be stated if fully set forth in the articles of incorporation; and

(b) increase or decrease the aggregate number of shares or the number of shares of, or eliminate and remove from the articles of incorporation, a class or series of shares that the corporation has authority to issue, unless a provision has been included in the articles of incorporation of the corporation after September 1,1993, expressly prohibiting those actions by the board of directors. The board of directors may not:

(i) decrease the number of shares within a class or series to less than the number of shares of that class or series that are then outstanding; or

(ii) eliminate or remove from the articles of incorporation any reference to any class or series of which shares are then outstanding.

To establish a class or series, the board of directors shall adopt a resolution setting forth the designation of the class or series and fixing and determining the designations, preferences, limitations, and relative rights, including voting rights, of the class or series. In order to increase or decrease the number of shares of, or eliminate and remove from the articles of incorporation any reference to, a class or series of shares, the board of directors shall adopt a resolution fixing and determining the new number of shares of each class or series in which the number of shares is increased or decreased or eliminating the class or series and removing references to the class or series from the articles of incorporation. The shares of any eliminated series shall resume the status of authorized but unissued shares of the class of shares from which the series was established unless otherwise provided in the resolution or the articles of incorporation.

(2) Before the first issuance of any shares of a class or series established or increased or decreased by resolution adopted by the board of directors under Subsection (1) of this section, and in order to eliminate from the articles of incorporation a class or series of shares and all references to the class or series contained in the articles, the corporation shall file with the Secretary of State a statement setting forth:

(a) the name of the corporation;

(b) if the statement relates to the establishment of a class or series of shares, a copy of the resolution establishing and designating the class or series and fixing and determining the preferences, limitations, and relative rights of the class or series;

(c) if the statement relates to an increase or decrease in the number of shares of any class or series, a copy of the resolution fixing and determining the new number of shares of each class or series in which the number of shares is increased or decreased;

(d) if the statement relates to the elimination of a class or series of shares and to the removal of all references to the class or series from the articles of incorporation, a copy of the resolution eliminating the class or series and removing all references to the class or series from the articles of incorporation;

(e) the date of adoption of the resolution; and

(f) that the resolution was duly adopted by all necessary action on the part of the corporation.

(3) The statement shall be executed on behalf of the corporation by an officer. The original and a copy of the statement shall be delivered to the Secretary of State. If the Secretary of State finds that the statement conforms to law, when the appropriate filing fee is paid as provided by law, the Secretary of State shall:

(a) endorse on the original and the copy the word "Filed," and the month, day, and year of the filing of the statement;

(b) file the original in the Secretary of State's office; and

(c) return the copy to the corporation or its representative.

(4) On the filing of a statement by the Secretary of State, the resolution establishing and designating the class or series and fixing and determining the preferences, limitations, and relative rights of the class or series, the resolution fixing the new number of shares of each class or series in which the number of shares is increased or decreased, or the resolution eliminating a class or series and all references to the class or series from the articles of incorporation, as appropriate, becomes an amendment of the articles of incorporation. An amendment of the articles of incorporation effected as provided by this Article is not subject to the procedure to amend the articles contained in Article 4.02 of this Act.

* * *

Art. 2.15. Consideration for Shares

A. Shares having a par value may be issued for such consideration, expressed in dollars, not less than the par value thereof, as shall be fixed from time to time by the board of directors.

B. Shares without par value may be issued for such consideration, expressed in dollars, as may be fixed from time to time by the board of directors, unless the articles of incorporation reserve to the shareholders the right to fix the consideration. In the event that such right reserved as to any shares, the shareholders shall, prior to the issuance of such shares, fix the consideration to be received for such shares, by a vote of the holders of a majority of all shares entitled to vote thereon.

C. Treasury shares may be disposed of by the corporation for such consideration as may be fixed from time to time by the board of directors.

D. That part of the surplus of a corporation which is transferred to stated capital upon the issuance of shares as a share dividend shall be deemed to be the consideration for the issuance of such shares.

E. In the event of the issuance of shares by a corporation upon the conversion or exchange of its indebtedness or shares, the consideration for the shares so issued shall be:

(1) The principal sum of, and accrued interest on, the indebtedness so exchanged or converted, or the stated capital then represented by the shares so exchanged or converted, and

(2) That part of surplus, if any, transferred to stated capital upon the issuance of shares for the shares so exchanged or converted, and

(3) Any additional consideration paid to the corporation upon the issuance of shares for the indebtedness or shares so exchanged or converted.

F. In the event of the issuance of shares by a corporation upon the exercise of rights or options entitling the holders thereof to purchase or receive from the corporation any of its shares, the consideration for the shares so issued shall be:

(1) The consideration, if any, received by the corporation for such rights or options, and

(2) The consideration, if any, received by the corporation for the issuance of shares upon the exercise of such rights or options.

Art. 2.16. Payment for Shares

A. Subject to any provision of the Constitution of the State of Texas to the contrary, the board of directors may authorize shares to be issued for consideration consisting of any tangible or intangible benefit to the corporation, including cash, promissory notes services performed, contracts for services to be performed, or other securities of the corporation. Shares may not be issued until the full amount of the consideration, fixed as provided by law, has been paid. When such consideration shall have been paid to the corporation or to a corporation of which all of the outstanding shares of each class are owned by the corporation, the shares shall be deemed to have been issued and the subscriber or shareholder entitled to receive such issue shall be a shareholder with respect to such shares, and the shares shall be considered fully paid and non-assessable.

B. In the absence of fraud in the transaction, the judgment of the board of directors or the shareholders, as the case may be, as to the value of the consideration received for shares shall be conclusive.

Art. 2.18. Expenses of Organization, Reorganization, and Financing

A. The reasonable charges and expenses of organization or reorganization of a corporation, and the reasonable expenses of and compensation for the sale or underwriting of its shares, may be paid or allowed by such corporation out of the consideration received by it in payment for its shares without thereby rendering such shares not fully paid and non-assessable.

Art. 2.19. Certificates Representing Shares

A. A corporation shall deliver certificates representing shares to which shareholders are entitled, or the shares of a corporation may be uncertificated shares. Unless otherwise provided by the articles of incorporation or bylaws, the board of directors of a corporation may provide by resolution that some or all of any or all classes and series of its shares shall be uncertificated shares, provided that such resolution shall not apply to shares represented by a certificate until such certificate is surrendered to the corporation. Certificates representing shares shall be signed by such officer or officers as the bylaws of the corporation shall prescribe, and may be sealed with the seal of the corporation or a facsimile thereof. The signatures of such officer or officers as the bylaws of the corporation shall prescribe upon a certificate may be facsimiles. In case any officer who has signed or whose facsimile signature has been placed upon such certificate shall have ceased to be such officer before such certificate is issued, it may be issued by the corporation with the same effect as if he were such officer at the date of its issuance.

B. In the event a corporation is authorized to issue shares of more than one class or series, each certificate representing shares issued by such corporation
(1) shall conspicuously set forth on the face or back of the certificate a full statement of all the designations, preferences, limitations, and relative rights of the shares of each class or series to the extent they have been fixed and determined and the authority of the board of directors to fix and determine the designations, preferences, limitations, and relative rights of subsequent series; or (2) shall conspicuously state on the face or back of the certificate that (a) such a statement is set forth in the articles of incorporation on file in the office of the Secretary of State and (b) the corporation will furnish a copy of such statement to the record holder of the certificate without charge on written request to the corporation at its principal place of business or registered office. In the event a corporation has by its articles of incorporation limited or denied the preemptive right of shareholders to acquire unissued or treasury shares of the corporation, each certificate representing shares issued by such corporation (1) shall conspicuously set forth on the face or back of the certificate a full statement of the limitation or denial of preemptive rights contained in the articles of incorporation, or (2) shall conspicuously state on the face or back of the certificate that (a) such a statement is set forth in the articles of incorporation on file in the office of the Secretary of State and (b) the corporation will furnish a copy of such statement to the record holder of the certificate without charge on request to the corporation at its principal place of business or registered office.

C. Each certificate representing shares shall state upon the face thereof:
(1) That the corporation is organized under the laws of this State.
(2) The name of the person to whom issued.
(3) The number and class of shares and the designation of the series, if any, which such certificate represents.
(4) The par value of each share represented by such certificate, or a statement that the shares are without par value.

D. In accordance with Chapter 8, Business & Commerce Code, a corporation shall, after the issuance or transfer of uncertificated shares, send to the registered owner of uncertificated shares a written notice containing the information required to be set forth or stated on certificates pursuant this Act. Except as otherwise expressly provided by law, the rights and obligations of the holders of uncertificated shares and the rights and obligations of the holders of certificates representing shares of the same class and series shall be identical. No share shall be issued until the consideration therefor, fixed as provided by law, has been fully paid.

E. No requirement of this Act with respect to matters to be set forth on certificates representing shares of a corporation shall apply to or affect certificates outstanding, when such requirement first becomes applicable to such certificates; but such requirements shall apply to all certificates thereafter issued whether in connection with an original issue of shares, a transfer of shares or otherwise. No certificate representing shares in which any provision of the articles of incorporation, or by-laws, or resolution, or agreement restricting the transfer of shares, shall have been incorporated by reference pursuant to the provisions of Section F of this Article prior to its amendment shall be invalidated or affected by such amendment; but such incorporation by reference shall not be used on certificates hereafter issued whether in connection with an original issue of shares, a transfer of shares, or otherwise.

F. Repealed by Acts 1975, 64th Leg., p. 322, ch. 134, § 22, eff. Sept. 1, 1975.

G. In the event any restriction on the transfer, or registration of the transfer, of shares shall be imposed or agreed to by the corporation, as permitted by this Act, each certificate representing shares so restricted (1) shall conspicuously set forth a full or summary statement of the restriction on the face of the certificate, or (2) shall set forth such statement on the back of the certificate and conspicuously refer to the same on the face of the certificate, or (3) shall conspicuously state on the face or back of the certificate that such a restriction exists pursuant to a specified document and (a) that the corporation will furnish to the record holder of the certificate without charge upon written request to the corporation at its principal place of business or registered office a copy of the specified document, or (b) if such document is one required or permitted to be and has been filed under this Act, that such specified document is on file in the office of the Secretary of State and contains a full statement of such restriction. Unless such document was on file in the office of the Secretary of State at the time of the request, a corporation which fails within a reasonable time to furnish the record holder of a certificate upon such request and without charge a copy of the specified document shall not be permitted thereafter to enforce its rights under the restriction imposed on the shares represented by such certificate.

Art. 2.20. Issuance of Fractional Shares or Scrip

A. A corporation may (1) issue fractions of a share, either represented by a certificate or uncertificated, (2) arrange for the disposition of fractional interests by those entitled thereto, (3) pay in cash the fair value of fractions of a share as of the time when those entitled to receive such fractions are determined, or (4) issue scrip in registered or bearer form which shall entitle the holder to receive a certificate for a full share or an uncertificated full share upon the surrender of such scrip aggregating a full share. A certificate for a fractional share or an uncertificated fractional share shall, but scrip shall not unless otherwise provided therein, entitle the holder to exercise voting rights, to receive dividends thereon, and to participate in any of the assets of the corporation in the event of liquidation. The board of directors may cause scrip to be issued subject to the condition that it shall become void if not exchanged for certificates representing full shares or uncertificated full shares before a specified date, or subject to the condition that the shares for which such scrip is exchangeable may be sold by the corporation and the proceeds thereof distributed to the holders of scrip, or subject to any other conditions which the board of directors may determine advisable.

Art. 2.42. Officers

A. The officers of a corporation shall consist of a president and a secretary, each of whom shall be elected by the board of directors at such time and in such manner as may be prescribed by the bylaws. Such other officers, including assistant officers, and agents as may be deemed necessary may be elected or appointed by the board of directors or chosen in such other manner as may be prescribed by the bylaws. Any two (2) or more offices may be held by the same person.

B. All officers and agents of the corporation, as between themselves and the corporation, shall have such authority and perform such duties in the management of the corporation as may be provided in the bylaws, or as may be determined by resolution of the board of directors not inconsistent with the bylaws.

C. In the discharge of any duty imposed or power conferred upon an officer, of a corporation the officer may in good faith and ordinary care rely on information, opinions, reports, or statement, including financial statements and other financial data, concerning the corporation or another person, that were prepared or presented by:

(1) one or more other officers or employees of the corporation including members of the board of directors; or

(2) legal counsel, public accountants, investment bankers, or other persons as to matters the officer reasonably believes are within the person's professional or expert competence.

An officer is not relying on good faith within the meaning of this section if the officer has knowledge concerning the matter in question that makes reliance otherwise permitted by this subsection unwarranted.

Art. 2.43. Removal of Officers

A. Any officer or agent or member of a committee elected or appointed by the board of directors may be removed by the board of directors whenever in its judgment the best interests of the corporation will be served thereby, but such removal shall be without prejudice to the contract rights, if any, of the person so removed. Election or appointment of an officer or agent or member of a committee shall not of itself create contract rights.

Art. 2.44. Books and Records

A. Each corporation shall keep books and records of account and shall keep minutes of the proceedings of its shareholders, its board of directors, and each committee of its board of directors. Each corporation shall keep at its registered office or principal place of business, or at the office of its transfer agent or registrar, a record of the original issuance of shares issued by the corporation and a record of each transfer of those shares that have been presented to the corporation for registration of transfer. Such records shall contain the names and addresses of all past and current shareholders of the corporation and the number and class or series of shares issued by the corporation held by each of them. Any books, records, minutes, and share transfer records may be in written form or in any other form capable of being converted into written form within a reasonable time. The principal place of business of a corporation, or the office of its transfer agent or registrar, may be located outside the State of Texas.

B. A director may examine the corporation's books and records of account, share transfer records, corporate minutes and any other corporate books and records for any purpose reasonably related to the director's service as a director. A court of competent jurisdiction may compel a corporation to open its books and records of account, share transfer records, corporate minutes or any other corporate books and records to permit the director to inspect the books or records and make copies or extracts from the books or records on a showing by a director that:

(1) he is a director;

(2) he demanded to inspect the corporate books and records;

(3) his purpose for inspecting the corporate books and records was reasonably related to his service as a director; and

(4) his right of access to the books and records was refused by the corporation.

The court may also award the director attorneys' fees and any other relief that the court deems just and proper.

C. Any person who shall have been a shareholder for at least six (6) months immediately preceding his demand, or shall be the holder of at least five per cent (5%) of all the outstanding shares of a corporation upon written demand stating the purpose thereof shall have the right to examine, in person or by agent accountant, or attorney, at any reasonable time or times, for any proper purpose, its relevant books and records of account, minutes, and share transfer records, and to make extracts therefrom.

D. Any corporation which shall refuse to allow any such shareholder or his agent, accountant or attorney, so to examine and make extracts from its books and records of account, minutes, and share transfer records, for any proper purpose, shall be liable to such shareholder for all costs and expenses, including attorneys' fees, incurred in enforcing his rights under this Article in addition to any other damages or remedy afforded him by law. It shall be a defense to any action for penalties under this section that the person suing therefor has within two (2) years sold or offered for sale any list of shareholders or of holders of voting trust certificates for shares of such corporation or any other corporation or has aided or abetted any person in procuring any list of shareholders or of holders of voting trust certificates for any such purpose, or has improperly used any information secured through any prior examination of the books and records of account, minutes, or share transfer records of such corporation or any other corporation, or was not acting in good faith or for a proper purpose in making his demand.

E. Nothing herein contained shall impair the power of any court of competent jurisdiction, upon proof of proper purpose by a beneficial or record holder of shares, irrespective of the period of time during which such holder shall have been a beneficial or record holder and irrespective of the number of shares held by him, to compel the production for examination by such holder of the books and records of account, minutes, and share transfer records of a corporation.

F. Upon the written request of any shareholder of a corporation, the corporation shall mail to such share holder its annual statements for its last fiscal year showing in reasonable detail its assets and liabilities and the results of its operations and the most recent interim statements, if any, which have been filed in a public record or otherwise published. The corporation shall be allowed a reasonable time to prepare such annual statements.

G. A holder of a beneficial interest in a voting trust entered into pursuant to Article 2.30 of this Act all be regarded as a holder of the shares represented by such beneficial interest for the purposes of this Article.

Form F. Minutes of Organizational Meeting

MINUTES OF THE ORGANIZATIONAL MEETING OF

DIRECTORS OF

Xeron Corporation

The organization meeting of the above corporation was held on January 29, , 1994 at 123 Main Street, Dallas, TX at 1 o'clock p. m.

The following persons were present:
John Smith
Mary Smith

The waiver of notice of this meeting was signed by all directors and incorporators named in the Articles of Incorporation and filed in the minute book.

The meeting was called to order by John Smith an incorporator named in the Articles of Incorporation. John Smith was nominated and elected Chairman and acted as such until relieved by the president. Mary Smith was nominated and elected temporary secretary, and acted as such until relieved by the permanent secretary.

A copy of the Articles of Incorporation which had been filed with the Secretary of State of the State of Texas on January 10 , 19 95 was examined by the directors and filed in the minute book.

The election of officers for the coming year was then taken up and the following were duly nominated and elected by the Board of Directors to be the officers of the corporation to serve until such time as their successors are elected and qualified:

President: John Smith
Vice President: Mary Smith
Secretary: Mary Smith
Treasurer: John Smith

The proposed bylaws for the corporation were then presented to the meeting and discussed. Upon motion duly made, seconded and carried, the Bylaws were adopted and added to the minute book.

Form A. Articles of Incorporation

ARTICLES OF INCORPORATION

OF

XERON CORPORATION

The undersigned, acting as the incorporator of a corporation under the Texas Business Corporation Act, hereby adopts the following Articles of Incorporation for such corporation:

ARTICLE ONE

The name of the corporation (the "Corporation") is XERON CORPORATION .

ARTICLE TWO

The period of the Corporation's duration is perpetual.

ARTICLE THREE

The purpose for which the Corporation is organized is to transact any or all lawful business for which corporations may be incorporated under the Texas Business Corporation Act.

ARTICLE FOUR

The Corporation shall have authority to issue 1,000,000 shares of capital stock. All of such shares shall be common stock, xxxxxxxxxxxxx/ par value $0.001 per share, have identical rights and privileges in every respect.

ARTICLE FIVE

The Corporation will not commence business until it has received for the issuance of its shares consideration the aggregate value of which is equal to at least $1,000.00, consisting of money, labor done or property actually received.

ARTICLE SIX

The address of the Corporation's initial registered office in the State of Texas is 123 Main St., Dallas, TX 75222 . The name of the Corporation's initial registered agent at such address is John Smith

ARTICLE SEVEN

The initial Board of Directors of the Corporation shall consist of 2 members who shall serve until the first annual meeting of shareholders and until their successors are elected and qualified. The names and mailing addresses of the persons who shall serve as the initial directors of the Corporation are as follows:
John Smith, Dallas, Texas
Mary Smith, Dallas, Texas

ARTICLE EIGHT

The name and mailing address of the incorporator of the Corporation is John Smith, 123 Main St., Dallas, TX 75222 .

IN WITNESS WHEREOF, the undersigned, a natural person of the age of 18 years or more and the incorporator hereinabove named, does hereby execute these Articles of Incorporation this 15th day of January, 1995 .

John Smith
Incorporator

A corporate seal for the corporation was then presented to the meeting and upon motion duly made, seconded and carried, it was adopted as the seal of the corporation. An impression thereof was then made in the margin of these minutes   (SEAL)

The necessity of opening a bank account was then discussed and upon motion duly made, seconded and carried, the following resolution was adopted:

RESOLVED that the corporation open bank accounts with Ezemoni Bank and that the officers of the corporation are authorized to take such action as is necessary to open such accounts; that the bank's printed form of resolution is hereby adopted and incorporated into these minutes by reference and shall be placed in the minute book; that any 1 of the following persons shall have signature authority over the account:

John Smith   Mary Smith

Proposed stock certificates and stock transfer ledger were then presented to the meeting and examined. Upon motion duly made, seconded and carried, the stock certificates and ledger were adopted as the certificates and transfer book to be used by the corporation. A sample stock certificate marked "VOID" and the stock transfer ledger were then added to the minute book. Upon motion duly made, seconded and carried, it was then resolved that the stock certificates when issued would be signed by the President and the Secretary of the corporation.

The tax status of the corporation was then discussed and it was moved, seconded and carried that the stock of the corporation be issued under §1244 of the Internal Revenue Code and that the officers of the corporation take the necessary action to:

1. Obtain an employer tax number by filing form SS-4

2. [X] Become an S-Corporation for tax purposes
    [ ] Remain a C-Corporation for tax purposes

The expenses of organizing the corporation were then discussed and it was moved, seconded and carried that the corporation pay in full from the corporate funds the expenses and reimburse any advances made by the incorporators upon proof of payment.

The directors named in the Articles of Incorporation then tendered their resignations, effective upon the adjournment of this meeting. Upon motion duly made, seconded and carried, the following named persons were elected as directors of the corporation each to hold office until the first annual meeting of shareholders, and until a successor of each shall have been elected and qualified.

John Smith
Mary Smith

There were presented to the corporation, the following offer(s) to purchase shares of capital stock:

FROM	NO. OF SHARES	CONSIDERATION
John Smith and Mary Smith, his wife, as joint tenants with full rights of survivorship	1,000,000	$1,000

The offers were discussed and after motion duly made, seconded and carried, were approved. It was further resolved that the Board of Directors has determined that the consideration was valued at least equal to the value of the shares to be issued and that upon tender of the consideration, fully paid non-assessable shares of the corporation be issued.

There being no further business before the meeting, on motion duly made, seconded and carried, the meeting adjourned.

DATED: January 29, 1995

John Smith
President

Mary Smith
Secretary

Part III Selection of Fiscal Tax Year (All corporations using this part must complete item O and one of items P, Q, or R.)

O   Check the applicable box below to indicate whether the corporation is:

1. ☐ A new corporation adopting the tax year entered in item I, Part I.
2. ☐ An existing corporation retaining the tax year entered in item I, Part I.
3. ☐ An existing corporation changing to the tax year entered in item I, Part I.

P   Complete item P if the corporation is using the expeditious approval provisions of Revenue Procedure 87-32, 1987-2 C.B. 396, to request (1) a natural business year (as defined in section 4.01(1) of Rev. Proc. 87-32), or (2) a year that satisfies the ownership tax year test in section 4.01(2) of Rev. Proc. 87-32. Check the applicable box below to indicate the representation statement the corporation is making as required under section 4 of Rev. Proc. 87-32.

1. Natural Business Year ▶ ☐   I represent that the corporation is retaining or changing to a tax year that coincides with its natural business year as defined in section 4.01(1) of Rev. Proc. 87-32 and as verified by its satisfaction of the requirements of section 4.02(1) of Rev. Proc. 87-32. In addition, if the corporation is changing to a natural business year as defined in section 4.01(1), I further represent that such tax year results in less deferral of income to the owners than the corporation's present tax year. I also represent that the corporation is not described in section 3.01(2) of Rev. Proc. 87-32. (See instructions for additional information that must be attached.)

2. Ownership Tax Year ▶ ☐   I represent that shareholders (as of the first day of the tax year to which the request relates) holding more than half of the shares of the stock (as of that first day) of the corporation have the same tax year or are concurrently changing to the tax year that the corporation adopts, retains, or changes to per item I, Part I. I also represent that the corporation is not described in section 3.01(2) of Rev. Proc. 87-32.

Note: If you do not use item P and the corporation wants a fiscal tax year, complete either item Q or R below. Item Q is used to request a fiscal tax year based on a business purpose and to make a back-up section 444 election.

Q   Business Purpose—To request a fiscal tax year based on a business purpose, you must check box Q1 and pay a user fee. See instructions for details. You may also check box Q2 and/or box Q3.

1. Check here ▶ ☐   if the fiscal year entered in item I, Part I, is requested under the provisions of section 6.03 of Rev. Proc. 87-32. Attach to Form 2553 a statement showing the business purpose for the requested fiscal year. See instructions for additional information that must be attached.

2. Check here ▶ ☐   to show that the corporation intends to make a back-up section 444 election in the event the corporation's business purpose request is not approved by the IRS. (See instructions for more information.)

3. Check here ▶ ☐   to show that the corporation agrees to adopt or change to a tax year ending December 31 if necessary for the IRS to accept this election for S corporation status in the event (1) the corporation's business purpose request is not approved and the corporation makes a back-up section 444 election, but is ultimately not qualified to make a section 444 election, or (2) the corporation's business purpose request is not approved and the corporation did not make a back-up section 444 election.

R   Section 444 Election—To make a section 444 election, you must check box R1 and you may also check box R2.

1. Check here ▶ ☐   to show the corporation will make, if qualified, a section 444 election to have the fiscal tax year shown in item I, Part I. To make the election, you must complete Form 8716, Election To Have a Tax Year Other Than a Required Tax Year, and either attach it to Form 2553 or file it separately.

2. Check here ▶ ☐   to show that the corporation agrees to adopt or change to a tax year ending December 31 if necessary for the IRS to accept this election for S corporation status in the event the corporation's ultimately not qualified to make a section 444 election.

Part III Qualified Subchapter S Trust (QSST) Election Under Section 1361(d)(2)**

Income beneficiary's name and address		Social security number

Trust's name and address		Employer identification number

Date on which stock of the corporation was transferred to the trust (month, day, year) ▶ ....

In order for the trust named above to be a QSST and thus a qualifying shareholder of the S corporation for which this Form 2553 is filed, I hereby make the election under section 1361(d)(2). Under penalties of perjury, I certify that the trust meets the definitional requirements of section 1361(d)(3) and that all other information provided in Part III is true, correct, and complete.

Signature of income beneficiary or signature and title of legal representative or other qualified person making the election		Date

**Use of Part III to make the QSST election may be made only if stock of the corporation has been transferred to the trust on or before the date on which the corporation makes its election to be an S corporation. The QSST election must be made and filed separately if stock of the corporation is transferred to the trust after the date on which the corporation makes the S election.

*U.S. Government Printing Office: 1993 — 301-826/82216

[A box over the form reads:]

For corporations on a calendar year basis, this side does not have to be filled in.

Election by a Small Business Corporation
(Under section 1362 of the Internal Revenue Code)
▶ For Paperwork Reduction Act Notice, see page 1 of instructions.
▶ See separate instructions.

OMB No. 1545-0146
Expires 8-31-96

Notes: 1. This election, to be an "S corporation," can be accepted only if all the tests are met under Who May Elect on page 1 of the instructions; all signatures in Parts I and III are originals (no photocopies) and the exact name and address of the corporation and other required form information are provided.

2. Do not file Form 1120S, U.S. Income Tax Return for an S Corporation, until you are notified that your election is accepted.

Part I Election Information

	Name of corporation (see instructions)	A Employer identification number (EIN)
Please Type or Print	XERON CORPORATION	59 : 1234567
	Number, street, and room or suite no. (If a P.O. box, see instructions)	B Date incorporated
	123 MAIN STREET	JAN. 29, 1995
	City or town, state, and ZIP code	C State of incorporation
	DALLAS, TX 75222	TEXAS

D   Election is to be effective for tax year beginning (month, day, year) ▶ 1 / 29 / 95

E   Name and title of officer or legal representative who the IRS may call for more information   JOHN SMITH, PRESIDENT

F   Telephone number of officer or legal representative (800) 555-1212

G   If the corporation changed its name or address after applying for the EIN shown in A, check the box ▶ ☐

H   If this election takes effect for the first tax year the corporation exists, enter month, day, and year of the earliest of the following: (1) date the corporation first had shareholders, (2) date the corporation first had assets, or (3) date the corporation began doing business ▶ 1 / 29 / 95

I   Selected tax year: Annual return will be filed for tax year ending (month and day) ▶ DEC. 31.

If the tax year ends on any date other than December 31, except for a 52-53-week tax year ending with reference to the month of December, you must complete Part II on the back. If the date you enter is the ending date of an automatic 52-53-week tax year, write "52-53-week year" to the right of the date. See Temporary Regulations section 1.441-2T(e)(3).

J Name and address of each shareholder; shareholder's spouse having a community property interest in the corporation's stock; and each tenant in common, joint tenant, and tenant by the entirety. (A husband and wife (and their estates) are counted as one shareholder in determining the number of shareholders without regard to the manner in which the stock is owned.)	K Shareholders' Consent Statement. Under penalties of perjury, we consent to the election of the above-named corporation to be an "S corporation" under section 1362(a) and that we have examined this consent statement, including accompanying schedules and statements, and to the best of our knowledge and belief, it is true, correct, and complete. (Shareholders sign and date below.)		L Stock owned		M Social security number or employer identification number (see instructions)	N Share-holders' tax year ends (month and day)
	Signature	Date	Number of shares	Dates acquired		
JOHN SMITH AND MARY SMITH AS JTWRS	*John Smith* *Mary Smith*	1/29/95	1,000,000	1/29/95	123-45-6789 234-56-7890	12/31 12/31

*For this election to be valid, the consent of each shareholder, shareholder's spouse having a community property interest in the corporation's stock, and each tenant in common, joint tenant, and tenant by the entirety must either appear above or be attached to this form. (See instructions for Column K if a continuation sheet or a separate consent statement is needed.)

Under penalties of perjury, I declare that I have examined this election, including accompanying schedules and statements, and to the best of my knowledge and belief, it is true, correct, and complete.

Signature of officer ▶ *John Smith*   Title ▶ PRESIDENT   Date ▶ 1/29/95

See Parts II and III on back.   Cat. No. 18629R

Form J. Offer to Purchase Stock

Offer to Purchase Stock

Date: January 29, 1995

To the Board of Directors of

XERON CORPORATION

The undersigned, hereby offers to purchase 1,000,000 shares of the common _____ stock of your corporation at a total purchase price of one thousand dollars in cash

Very truly yours,

John and Mary Smith

Offer to Sell Stock
Pursuant to Sec. 1244 I.R.C.

Date: January 29, 1995

To: John and Mary Smith

Dear John and Mary Smith

The corporation hereby offers to sell to you 1,000,000 shares of its common stock at a price of $ 0.001 per share. These shares are issued pursuant to Section 1244 of the Internal Revenue Code,

Your signature below shall constitute an acceptance of our offer as of the date it is received by the corporation.

Very truly yours,

XERON CORPORATION

By: _____

Accepted: _____

Form **SS-4** (Rev. December 1993) Department of the Treasury Internal Revenue Service	**Application for Employer Identification Number** (For use by employers, corporations, partnerships, trusts, estates, churches, government agencies, certain individuals, and others. See instructions.)	EIN	OMB No. 1545-0003 Expires 12-31-96

Please type or print clearly.

1 Name of applicant (Legal name) (See instructions.)
XERON CORPORATION

2 Trade name of business, if different from name in line 1

3 Executor, trustee, "care of" name

4a Mailing address (street address) (room, apt., or suite no.)
P.O. BOX 222

4b City, state, and ZIP code
DALLAS, TEXAS 75222

5a Business address, if different from address in lines 4a and 4b
123 MAIN STREET

5b City, state, and ZIP code
DALLAS, TEXAS 75222

6 County and state where principal business is located
DALLAS, TEXAS

7 Name of principal officer, general partner, grantor, owner, or trustor—SSN required (See instructions.) ▶
JOHN SMITH

8a Type of entity (Check only one box.) (See instructions.)
☐ Sole Proprietor (SSN) _____
☐ REMIC
☐ State/local government
☐ Other nonprofit organization (specify) _____
☐ Other (specify) ▶ _____
☐ Personal service corp.
☐ National guard
☐ Estate (SSN of decedent) _____
☐ Plan administrator-SSN _____
☒ Other corporation (specify) ▶ Retail store
☐ Federal government/military _____
(enter GEN if applicable)
☐ Trust
☐ Partnership
☐ Farmers' cooperative
☐ Church or church controlled organization

8b If a corporation, name the state or foreign country (if applicable) where incorporated
State: TEXAS   Foreign country: _____

9 Reason for applying (Check only one box.)
☒ Started new business (specify) ▶ Retail store
☐ Hired employees
☐ Created a pension plan (specify type) ▶ _____
☐ Banking purpose (specify) ▶ _____
☐ Changed type of organization (specify) ▶ _____
☐ Purchased going business
☐ Created a trust (specify) ▶ _____
☐ Other (specify) ▶ _____

10 Date business started or acquired (Mo., day, year) (See instructions.)
1/29/95

11 Enter closing month of accounting year. (See instructions.)
DECEMBER

12 First date wages or annuities were paid or will be paid (Mo., day, year). Note: If applicant is a withholding agent, enter date income will first be paid to nonresident alien. (Mo., day, year)
2/5/95

13 Enter highest number of employees expected in the next 12 months. Note: If the applicant does not expect to have any employees during the period, enter "0-".
Nonagricultural: 3   Agricultural: ____   Household: ____

14 Principal activity (See instructions.) ▶ Retail clothing store

15 Is the principal business activity manufacturing? ☐ Yes ☒ No
If "Yes," principal product and raw material used ▶

16 To whom are most of the products or services sold? Please check the appropriate box.
☒ Public (retail) ☐ Business (wholesale) ☐ Business (retail) ☐ Other (specify) ▶

17a Has the applicant ever applied for an identification number for this or any other business? ☐ Yes ☒ No
Note: If "Yes," please complete lines 17b and 17c.

17b If you checked the "Yes" box in line 17a, give applicant's legal name and trade name, if different than name shown on prior application.
Legal name ▶ _____   Trade name ▶ _____

17c Enter approximate date, city, and state where the application was filed and the previous employer identification number if known.
Approximate date when filed (Mo., day, year): ____   City and state where filed: ____   Previous EIN: ____

Under penalties of perjury, I declare that I have examined this application, and to the best of my knowledge and belief, it is true, correct, and complete.

Name and title (Please type or print clearly.) ▶ JOHN SMITH, PRESIDENT

Business telephone number (include area code): (800) 555-1212

Signature ▶ _John Smith_   Date ▶ 1/29/95

Note: Do not write below this line.	For official use only.		
Please leave blank ▶	Geo.	Ind.	Class	Size	Reason for applying

For Paperwork Reduction Act Notice, see attached instructions.   Cat. No. 16055N   Form **SS-4** (Rev. 12-93)

Appendix C
Forms

ARTICLES OF INCORPORATION

OF

_____

The undersigned, acting as the incorporator of a corporation under the Texas Business Corporation Act, hereby adopts the following Articles of Incorporation for such corporation:

ARTICLE ONE

The name of the corporation (the "Corporation") is

_____.

ARTICLE TWO

The period of the Corporation's duration is perpetual.

ARTICLE THREE

The purpose for which the Corporation is organized is to transact any or all lawful business for which corporations may be incorporated under the Texas Business Corporation Act.

ARTICLE FOUR

The Corporation shall have authority to issue shares of capital stock. All of such shares shall be common stock, without par value/ par value $_____ per share, and shall have identical rights and privileges in every respect.

ARTICLE FIVE

The Corporation will not commence business until it has received for the issuance of its shares consideration the aggregate value of which is equal to at least $1,000.00, consisting of money, labor done or property actually received.

ARTICLE SIX

The address of the Corporation's initial registered office in the State of Texas is _____.
The name of the Corporation's initial registered agent at such address is _____.

ARTICLE SEVEN

The initial Board of Directors of the Corporation shall consist of _____ members who shall serve until the first annual meeting of shareholders and until their successors are elected and qualified. The names and mailing addresses of the persons who shall serve as the initial directors of the Corporation are as follows:

ARTICLE EIGHT

The name and mailing address of the incorporator of the Corporation is _____

_____.

IN WITNESS WHEREOF, the undersigned, a natural person of the age of 18 years or more and the incorporator hereinabove named, does hereby execute these Articles of Incorporation this day of _____, 19_____.

_____
Incorporator

ARTICLES OF INCORPORATION

OF

_____

_____

The undersigned, acting as the incorporator of a corporation under the Texas Business Corporation Act, hereby adopts the following Articles of Incorporation for such corporation:

ARTICLE ONE

The name of the corporation (the "Corporation") is

_____.

ARTICLE TWO

The corporation is a professional corporation.

ARTICLE THREE

The period of the Corporation's duration is perpetual.

ARTICLE FOUR

The purpose for which the Corporation is organized is

_____.

ARTICLE FIVE

The Corporation shall have authority to issue

shares of capital stock. All of such shares shall be common stock, without par value/ par value $_____ per share, and shall have identical rights and privileges in every respect.

ARTICLE SIX

The Corporation will not commence business until it has received for the issuance of its shares consideration the aggregate value of which is equal to at least $1,000.00, consisting of money, labor done or property actually received.

ARTICLE SEVEN

The address of the Corporation's initial registered office in the State of Texas is _____.

The name of the Corporation's initial registered agent at such address is _____.

ARTICLE EIGHT

The initial Board of Directors of the Corporation shall consist of _____ members who shall serve until the first annual meeting of shareholders and until their successors are elected and qualified. The names and mailing addresses of the persons who shall serve as the initial directors of the Corporation are as follows:

ARTICLE NINE

The name and mailing address of the incorporator of the Corporation is _____

_____.

IN WITNESS WHEREOF, the undersigned, a natural person of the age of 18 years or more and the incorporator hereinabove named, does hereby execute these Articles of Incorporation this day of _____, 19____.

_____
Incorporator

TRANSMITTAL LETTER

Corporations Section
Statutory Filings Division
Office of the Secretary of State
P.O. Box 13697
Austin, TX 78711-3697

SUBJECT: _____
(Proposed corporate name – must include suffix)

Enclosed is an original and one (1) copy of the articles of incorporation and a check for:

☐ $300.00   ☐ $310.00   ☐ $307.00

Filing Fee   Filing Fee   Filing Fee
                      & Special   & Certified Copy
                      Handling

Please return the photocopy to me with the filing date stamped on it.

FROM: _____
                    Name (printed or typed)

         _____
                    Address

         _____
                    City, State & Zip

         _____
                    Daytime Telephone Number

Form D. IRS Form SS-4

Form SS-4
(Rev. December 1993)
Department of the Treasury
Internal Revenue Service

Application for Employer Identification Number
(For use by employers, corporations, partnerships, trusts, estates, churches, government agencies, certain individuals, and others. See instructions.)

EIN

OMB No. 1545-0003
Expires 12-31-96

Please type or print clearly.

1 Name of applicant (Legal name) (See instructions.)

2 Trade name of business. if different from name in line 1

3 Executor, trustee, "care of" name

4a Mailing address (street address) (room, apt., or suite no.)

5a Business address, if different from address in lines 4a and 4b

4b City, state, and ZIP code

5b City, state, and ZIP code

6 County and state where principal business is located

7 Name of principal officer. general partner, grantor, owner, or trustor—SSN required (See instructions.) ▶

8a Type of entity (Check only one box.) (See instructions.)
☐ Sole Proprietor (SSN) _____
☐ REMIC   ☐ Personal service corp.
☐ State/local government   ☐ National guard
☐ Other nonprofit organization (specify) _____
☐ Other (specify) ▶ _____

☐ Estate (SSN of decedent) _____
☐ Plan administrator-SSN _____
☐ Other corporation (specify) _____
☐ Federal government/military   ☐ Church or church controlled organization
_____ (enter GEN if applicable) _____

☐ Trust
☐ Partnership
☐ Farmers' cooperative

8b If a corporation, name the state or foreign country (if applicable) where incorporated ▶

State

Foreign country

9 Reason for applying (Check only one box.)
☐ Started new business (specify) ▶ _____
☐ Hired employees
☐ Created a pension plan (specify type) ▶ _____
☐ Banking purpose (specify) ▶ _____

☐ Changed type of organization (specify) ▶ _____
☐ Purchased going business
☐ Created a trust (specify) ▶ _____
☐ Other (specify) ▶

10 Date business started or acquired (Mo., day, year) (See instructions.)

11 Enter closing month of accounting year. (See instructions.)

12 First date wages or annuities were paid or will be paid (Mo., day, year). **Note:** *If applicant is a withholding agent, enter date income will first be paid to nonresident alien. (Mo., day, year)* . . . . ▶

13 Enter highest number of employees expected in the next 12 months. **Note:** *If the applicant does not expect to have any employees during the period, enter "0."* . . . . ▶

Nonagricultural	Agricultural	Household

14 Principal activity (See instructions.) ▶

15 Is the principal business activity manufacturing? . . . . ☐ Yes   ☐ No
If "Yes," principal product and raw material used ▶

16 To whom are most of the products or services sold? Please check the appropriate box.
☐ Public (retail)   ☐ Other (specify) ▶
☐ Business (wholesale)   ☐ N/A

17a Has the applicant ever applied for an identification number for this or any other business? . . . . ☐ Yes   ☐ No
Note: *If "Yes," please complete lines 17b and 17c.*

17b If you checked the "Yes" box in line 17a, give applicant's legal name and trade name, if different than name shown on prior application.

Legal name ▶

Trade name ▶

17c Enter approximate date, city, and state where the application was filed and the previous employer identification number if known.
Approximate date when filed (Mo., day, year) | City and state where filed | Previous EIN

Under penalties of perjury, I declare that I have examined this application, and to the best of my knowledge and belief, it is true, correct, and complete.

Business telephone number (include area code)

Name and title (Please type or print clearly.) ▶

Signature ▶

Date ▶

Note: *Do not write below this line.   For official use only.*

Please leave blank ▶	Geo.	Ind.	Class	Size	Reason for applying

For Paperwork Reduction Act Notice, see attached instructions.

Cat. No. 16055N

Form **SS-4** (Rev. 12-93)

79

General Instructions

(Section references are to the Internal Revenue Code unless otherwise noted.)

Purpose

Use Form SS-4 to apply for an employer identification number (EIN). An EIN is a nine-digit number (for example, 12-3456789) assigned to sole proprietors, corporations, partnerships, estates, trusts, and other entities for filing and reporting purposes. The information you provide on this form will establish your filing and reporting requirements.

Who Must File

You must file this form if you have not obtained an EIN before and

• You pay wages to one or more employees.

• You are required to have an EIN to use on any return, statement, or other document, even if you are not an employer.

• You are a withholding agent required to withhold taxes on income, other than wages, paid to a nonresident alien (individual, corporation, partnership, etc.). A withholding agent may be an agent, broker, fiduciary, manager, tenant, or spouse, and is required to file **Form 1042**, Annual Withholding Tax Return for U.S. Source Income of Foreign Persons.

• You file **Schedule C**, Profit or Loss From Business, or **Schedule F**, Profit or Loss From Farming, of **Form 1040**, U.S. Individual Income Tax Return, and have a Keogh plan or are required to file excise, employment, or alcohol, tobacco, or firearms returns.

The following must use EINs even if they do not have any employees:

• Trusts, except the following:

1. Certain grantor-owned revocable trusts (see the Instructions for Form 1040).

2. Individual Retirement Arrangement (IRA) trusts, unless the trust has to file **Form 990-T**, Exempt Organization Business Income Tax Return (See the Instructions for Form 990-T.)

• Estates

• Partnerships

• REMICS (real estate mortgage investment conduits) (See the instructions for **Form 1066**, U.S. Real Estate Mortgage Investment Conduit Income Tax Return.)

• Corporations

• Nonprofit organizations (churches, clubs, etc.)

• Farmers' cooperatives

• Plan administrators (A plan administrator is the person or group of persons specified as the administrator by the instrument under which the plan is operated.)

Note: *Household employers are not required to file Form SS-4 to get an EIN. An EIN may be assigned to you without filing Form SS-4 if your only employees are household employees (domestic workers) in your private home. To have an EIN assigned to you, write "NONE" in the space for the EIN on **Form 942**, Employer's Quarterly Tax Return for Household Employees, when you file it.*

When To Apply for A New EIN

New Business.—If you become the new owner of an existing business, **DO NOT** use the EIN of the former owner. If you already have an EIN, use that number. If you do not have an EIN, apply for one on this form. If you become the "owner" of a corporation by acquiring its stock, use the corporation's EIN.

Changes in Organization or Ownership.—If you already have an EIN, you may need to get a new one if either the organization or ownership of your business changes. If you incorporate a sole proprietorship or form a partnership, you must get a new EIN. However, **DO NOT** apply for a new EIN if you change only the name of your business.

File Only One Form SS-4.—File only one Form SS-4, regardless of the number of businesses operated or trade names under which a business operates. However, each corporation in an affiliated group must file a separate application.

EIN Applied For, But Not Received.—If you do not have an EIN by the time a return is due, write "Applied for" and the date you applied in the space shown for the number. **DO NOT** show your social security number as an EIN on returns.

If you do not have an EIN by the time a tax deposit is due, send your payment to the Internal Revenue service center for your filing area. (See **Where To Apply** below.) Make your check or money order payable to Internal Revenue Service and show your name (as shown on Form SS-4), address, kind of tax, period covered, and date you applied for an EIN.

For more information about EINs, see **Pub. 583**, Taxpayers Starting a Business and **Pub. 1635**, EINs Made Easy.

How To Apply

You can apply for an EIN either by mail or by telephone. You can get an EIN immediately by calling the Tele-TIN phone number for the service center for your state, or you can send the completed Form SS-4 directly to the service center to receive your EIN in the mail.

Application by Tele-TIN.—Under the Tele-TIN program, you can receive your EIN over the telephone and use it immediately to file a return or make a payment. To receive an EIN by phone, complete Form SS-4, then call the Tele-TIN phone number listed for your state under **Where To Apply.** The person making the call must be authorized to sign the form (see **Signature block** on page 3).

An IRS representative will use the information from the Form SS-4 to establish your account and assign you an EIN. Write the number you are given on the upper right-hand corner of the form, sign and date it.

*You should mail or FAX the signed SS-4 **within 24 hours** to the Tele-TIN Unit at the service center address for your state.* The IRS representative will give you the FAX number. The FAX numbers are also listed in Pub. 1635.

Taxpayer representatives can receive their client's EIN by phone if they first send a facsimile (FAX) of a completed **Form 2848**, Power of Attorney and Declaration of Representative, or **Form 8821**, Tax Information Authorization, to the Tele-TIN unit. The Form 2848 or Form 8821 will be used solely to release the EIN to the representative authorized on the form.

Application by Mail.—Complete Form SS-4 at least 4 to 5 weeks before you will need an EIN. Sign and date the application and mail it to the service center address for your state. You will receive your EIN in the mail in approximately 4 weeks.

Where To Apply

The Tele-TIN phone numbers listed below will involve a long-distance charge to callers outside of the local calling area, and should be used only to apply for an EIN. THE NUMBERS MAY CHANGE WITHOUT NOTICE. Use 1-800-829-1040 to verify a number or to ask about an application by mail or other Federal tax matters.

If your principal business, office or agency, or legal residence in the case of an individual, is located in:	Call the Tele-TIN phone number shown or file with the Internal Revenue Service center at:
Florida, Georgia, South Carolina	Attn: Entity Control Atlanta, GA 39901 (404) 455-2360
New Jersey, New York City and counties of Nassau, Rockland, Suffolk, and Westchester	Attn: Entity Control Holtsville, NY 00501 (516) 447-4955
New York (all other counties), Connecticut, Maine, Massachusetts, New Hampshire, Rhode Island, Vermont	Attn: Entity Control Andover, MA 05501 (508) 474-9717
Illinois, Iowa, Minnesota, Missouri, Wisconsin	Attn: Entity Control Stop 57A 2306 E. Bannister Rd. Kansas City, MO 64131 (816) 926-5999
Delaware, District of Columbia, Maryland, Pennsylvania, Virginia	Attn: Entity Control Philadelphia, PA 19255 (215) 574-2400

Indiana, Kentucky, Michigan, Ohio, West Virginia	Attn: Entity Control Cincinnati, OH 45999 (606) 292-5467
Kansas, New Mexico, Oklahoma, Texas	Attn: Entity Control Austin, TX 73301 (512) 462-7843
Alaska, Arizona, California (counties of Alpine, Amador, Butte, Calaveras, Colusa, Contra Costa, Del Norte, El Dorado, Glenn, Humboldt, Lake, Lassen, Marin, Mendocino, Modoc, Napa, Nevada, Placer, Plumas Sacramento, San Joaquin, Shasta, Sierra, Siskiyou, Solano, Sonoma, Sutter, Tehama, Trinity, Yolo, and Yuba), Colorado, Idaho, Montana, Nebraska, Nevada, North Dakota, Oregon, South Dakota, Utah, Washington, Wyoming	Attn: Entity Control Mail Stop 6271-T P.O. Box 9950 Ogden, UT 84409 (801) 620-7645
California (all other counties), Hawaii	Attn: Entity Control Fresno, CA 93888 (209) 452-4010
Alabama, Arkansas, Louisiana, Mississippi, North Carolina, Tennessee	Attn: Entity Control Memphis, TN 37501 (901) 365-5970

If you have no legal residence, principal place of business, or principal office or agency in any state, file your form with the Internal Revenue Service Center, Philadelphia, PA 19255 or call (215) 574-2400.

Specific Instructions

The instructions that follow are for those items that are not self-explanatory. Enter N/A (nonapplicable) on the lines that do not apply.

Line 1.—Enter the legal name of the entity applying for the EIN exactly as it appears on the social security card, charter, or other applicable legal document.

Individuals.—Enter the first name, middle initial, and last name.

Trusts.—Enter the name of the trust.

Estate of a decedent.—Enter the name of the estate.

Partnerships.—Enter the legal name of the partnership as it appears in the partnership agreement.

Corporations.—Enter the corporate name as set forth in the corporation charter or other legal document creating it.

Plan administrators.—Enter the name of the plan administrator. A plan administrator who already has an EIN should use that number.

Line 2.—Enter the trade name of the business if different from the legal name. The trade name is the "doing business as" name.

Note: *Use the full legal name on line 1 on all tax returns filed for the entity. However, if you enter a trade name on line 2 and choose to use the trade name instead of the legal name, enter the trade name on all returns you file. To prevent processing delays and errors, **always** use either the legal name only or the trade name only on all tax returns.*

Line 3.—Trusts enter the name of the trustee. Estates enter the name of the executor, administrator, or other fiduciary. If the entity applying has a designated person to receive tax information, enter that person's name as the "care of" person. Print or type the first name, middle initial, and last name.

Line 7.—Enter the first name, middle initial, last name, and social security number (SSN) of a principal officer if the business is a corporation; of a general partner if a partnership; and of a grantor owner, or trustor if a trust.

Line 8a.—Check the box that best describes the type of entity applying for the EIN. If not specifically mentioned, check the "other" box and enter the type of entity. Do not enter N/A.

Sole proprietor.—Check this box if you file Schedule C or F (Form 1040) and have a Keogh plan, or are required to file excise, employment, or alcohol, tobacco, or firearms returns. Enter your SSN (social security number) in the space provided.

Plan administrator.—If the plan administrator is an individual, enter the plan administrator's SSN in the space provided.

Withholding agent.—If you are a withholding agent required to file Form 1042, check the "other" box and enter "withholding agent."

REMICs.—Check this box if the entity has elected to be treated as a real estate mortgage investment conduit (REMIC). See the Instructions for Form 1066 for more information.

Personal service corporations.—Check this box if the entity is a personal service corporation. An entity is a personal service corporation for a tax year only if:

● The principal activity of the entity during the testing period (prior tax year) for the tax year is the performance of personal services substantially by employee-owners.

● The employee-owners own 10 percent of the fair market value of the outstanding stock in the entity on the last day of the testing period.

Personal services include performance of services in such fields as health, law, accounting, consulting, etc. For more information about personal service corporations, see the instructions to **Form 1120,** U.S. Corporation Income Tax Return, and **Pub. 542,** Tax Information on Corporations.

Other corporations.—This box is for any corporation other than a personal service corporation. If you check this box, enter the type of corporation (such as insurance company) in the space provided.

Other nonprofit organizations.—Check this box if the nonprofit organization is

other than a church or church-controlled organization and specify the type of nonprofit organization (for example, an educational organization.)

If the organization also seeks tax-exempt status, you must file either **Package 1023** or **Package 1024,** Application for Recognition of Exemption. Get **Pub. 557,** Tax-Exempt Status for Your Organization, for more information.

Group exemption number (GEN).—If the organization is covered by a group exemption letter, enter the four-digit GEN. (Do not confuse the GEN with the nine-digit EIN.) If you do not know the GEN, contact the parent organization. Get Pub. 557 for more information about group exemption numbers.

Line 9.—Check only **one** box. Do not enter N/A.

Started new business.—Check this box if you are starting a new business that requires an EIN. If you check this box, enter the type of business being started. **DO NOT** apply if you already have an EIN and are only adding another place of business.

Changed type of organization.—Check this box if the business is changing its type of organization, for example, if the business was a sole proprietorship and has been incorporated or has become a partnership. If you check this box, specify in the space provided the type of change made, for example, "from sole proprietorship to partnership."

Purchased going business.—Check this box if you purchased an existing business. DO NOT use the former owner's EIN. Use your own EIN if you already have one.

Hired employees.—Check this box if the existing business is requesting an EIN because it has hired or is hiring employees and is therefore required to file employment tax returns. **DO NOT** apply if you already have an EIN and are only hiring employees. If you are hiring household employees, see **Note** under **Who Must File** on page 2.

Created a trust.—Check this box if you created a trust, and enter the type of trust created.

Note: *DO NOT file this form if you are the individual-grantor/owner of a revocable trust. You must use your SSN for the trust. See the instructions for Form 1040.*

Created a pension plan.—Check this box if you have created a pension plan and need this number for reporting purposes. Also, enter the type of plan created.

Banking purpose.—Check this box if you are requesting an EIN for banking purposes only and enter the banking purpose (for example, a bowling league for depositing dues, an investment club for dividend and interest reporting, etc.).

Other (specify).—Check this box if you are requesting an EIN for any reason other than those for which there are checkboxes, and enter the reason.

Line 10.—If you are starting a new business, enter the starting date of the business. If the business you acquired is already operating, enter the date you acquired the business. Trusts should enter the date the trust was legally created. Estates should enter the date of death of the decedent whose name appears on line 1 or the date when the estate was legally funded.

Line 11.—Enter the last month of your accounting year or tax year. An accounting or tax year is usually 12 consecutive months, either a calendar year or a fiscal year (including a period of 52 or 53 weeks). A calendar year is 12 consecutive months ending on December 31. A fiscal year is either 12 consecutive months ending on the last day of any month other than December or a 52-53 week year. For more information on accounting periods, see **Pub. 538,** Accounting Periods and Methods.

Individuals.—Your tax year generally will be a calendar year.

Partnerships.—Partnerships generally must adopt the tax year of either (1) the majority partners; (2) the principal partners; (3) the tax year that results in the least aggregate (total) deferral of income; or (4) some other tax year. (See the Instructions for **Form 1065,** U.S. Partnership Return of Income, for more information.)

REMICs.—Remics must have a calendar year as their tax year.

Personal service corporations.—A personal service corporation generally must adopt a calendar year unless:

- It can establish a business purpose for having a different tax year, or

- It elects under section 444 to have a tax year other than a calendar year.

Trusts.—Generally, a trust must adopt a calendar year except for the following:

- Tax-exempt trusts,
- Charitable trusts, and
- Grantor-owned trusts.

Line 12.—If the business has or will have employees, enter the date on which the business began or will begin to pay wages. If the business does not plan to have employees, enter N/A.

Withholding agent.—Enter the date you began or will begin to pay income to a nonresident alien. This also applies to individuals who are required to file Form 1042 to report alimony paid to a nonresident alien.

Line 14.—Generally, enter the exact type of business being operated (for example, advertising agency, farm, food or beverage establishment, labor union, real estate agency, steam laundry, rental of coin-operated vending machine, investment club, etc.). Also state if the business will involve the sale or distribution of alcoholic beverages.

Governmental.—Enter the type of organization (state, county, school district, or municipality, etc.).

Nonprofit organization (other than governmental).—Enter whether organized for religious, educational, or humane purposes, and the principal activity (for example, religious organization—hospital, charitable).

Mining and quarrying.—Specify the process and the principal product (for example, mining bituminous coal, contract drilling for oil, quarrying dimension stone, etc.).

Contract construction.—Specify whether general contracting or special trade contracting. Also, show the type of work normally performed (for example, general contractor for residential buildings, electrical subcontractor, etc.).

Food or beverage establishments.—Specify the type of establishment and state whether you employ workers who receive tips (for example, lounge—yes).

Trade.—Specify the type of sales and the principal line of goods sold (for example, wholesale dairy products, manufacturer's representative for mining machinery, retail hardware, etc.).

Manufacturing.—Specify the type of establishment operated (for example, sawmill, vegetable cannery, etc.).

Signature block.—The application must be signed by: (1) the individual, if the applicant is an individual, (2) the president, vice president, or other principal officer, if the applicant is a corporation, (3) a responsible and duly authorized member or officer having knowledge of its affairs, if the applicant is a partnership or other unincorporated organization, or (4) the fiduciary, if the applicant is a trust or estate.

Some Useful Publications

You may get the following publications for additional information on the subjects covered on this form. To get these and other free forms and publications, call 1-800-TAX-FORM (1-800-829-3676).

Pub. 1635, EINs Made Easy

Pub. 538, Accounting Periods and Methods

Pub. 541, Tax Information on Partnerships

Pub. 542, Tax Information on Corporations

Pub. 557, Tax-Exempt Status for Your Organization

Pub. 583, Taxpayers Starting A Business

Pub. 937, Employment Taxes and Information Returns

Package 1023, Application for Recognition of Exemption

Package 1024, Application for Recognition of Exemption Under Section 501(a) or for Determination Under Section 120

Paperwork Reduction Act Notice

We ask for the information on this form to carry out the Internal Revenue laws of the United States. You are required to give us the information. We need it to ensure that you are complying with these laws and to allow us to figure and collect the right amount of tax.

The time needed to complete and file this form will vary depending on individual circumstances. The estimated average time is:

Recordkeeping	7 min.
Learning about the law or the form	18 min.
Preparing the form	44 min.
Copying, assembling, and sending the form to the IRS	20 min.

If you have comments concerning the accuracy of these time estimates or suggestions for making this form more simple, we would be happy to hear from you. You can write to both the **Internal Revenue Service,** Attention: Reports Clearance Officer, PC:FP, Washington, DC 20224; and the **Office of Management and Budget,** Paperwork Reduction Project (1545-0003), Washington, DC 20503. **DO NOT** send this form to either of these offices. Instead, see **Where To Apply** on page 2.

WAIVER OF NOTICE

OF THE ORGANIZATIONAL MEETING

OF

_____ _____

We, the undersigned directors named in the articles of incorporation of the above-named corporation hereby agree and consent that the organization meeting of the corporation be held on the date and time and place stated below and hereby waive all notice of such meeting and of any adjournment thereof.

Place of meeting: _____

Date of Meeting: _____

Time of meeting: _____

Dated: _____

_____

Director

_____

Director

_____

Director

MINUTES OF THE ORGANIZATIONAL MEETING OF

DIRECTORS OF

_____ _____

The organization meeting of the above corporation was held on
_____, 19____ at _____
_____ at ____ o'clock __m.

The following persons were present:

_____   _____
_____   _____
_____   _____

The waiver of notice of this meeting was signed by all directors
named in the Articles of Incorporation and filed in the minute book.

The meeting was called to order by _____,
a director named in the Articles of Incorporation. _____
_____was nominated and elected Chairman and acted as
such until relieved by the president. _____
was nominated and elected temporary secretary, and acted as such until
relieved by the permanent secretary.

A copy of the Articles of Incorporation which had been filed with
the Secretary of State of the State of Texas on _____,
19____ was examined by the directors and incorporators and filed in
the minute book.

The election of officers for the coming year was then taken up
and the following were duly nominated and elected by the Board of
Directors to be the officers of the corporation to serve until such
time as their successors are elected and qualified:

President: _____
Vice President: _____
Secretary: _____
Treasurer: _____

The proposed bylaws for the corporation were then presented to
the meeting and discussed. Upon motion duly made, seconded and carried,
the Bylaws were adopted and added to the minute book.

A corporate seal for the corporation was then presented to the meeting and upon motion duly made, seconded and carried, it was adopted as the seal of the corporation. An impression thereof was then made in the margin of these minutes

The necessity of opening a bank account was then discussed and upon motion duly made, seconded and carried the following resolution was adopted:

RESOLVED that the corporation open bank accounts with _____ _____ and that the officers of the corporation are authorized to take such action as is necessary to open such accounts; that the bank's printed form of resolution is hereby adopted and incorporated into these minutes by reference and shall be placed in the minute book; that any ____ of the following persons shall have signature authority over the account:

_____   _____
_____   _____
_____   _____

Proposed stock certificates and stock transfer ledger were then presented to the meeting and examined. Upon motion duly made, seconded and carried the stock certificates and ledger were adopted as the certificates and transfer book to be used by the corporation. A sample stock certificate marked "VOID" and the stock transfer ledger were then added to the minute book. Upon motion duly made, seconded and carried, it was then resolved that the stock certificates when issued would be signed by the President and the Secretary of the corporation.

The tax status of the corporation was then discussed and it was moved, seconded and carried that the stock of the corporation be issued under §1244 of the Internal Revenue Code and that the officers of the corporation take the necessary action to:

1.   Obtain an employer tax number by filing form SS-4

2.   ☐ Become an S-corporation for tax purposes
      ☐ Remain a C-corporation for tax purposes

The expenses of organizing the corporation were then discussed and it was moved, seconded and carried that the corporation pay in full from the corporate funds the expenses and reimburse any advances made by the incorporators upon proof of payment.

The directors named in the Articles of Incorporation then tendered their resignations, effective upon the adjournment of this meeting. Upon motion duly made, seconded and carried, the following named persons were elected as directors of the corporation each to hold office until the first annual meeting of shareholders, and until a successor of each shall have been elected and qualified.

_____

_____

_____

There were presented to the corporation, the following offer(s) to purchase shares of capital stock:

FROM	NO. OF SHARES	CONSIDERATION
_____	_____	_____
_____	_____	_____
_____	_____	_____
_____	_____	_____

The offers were discussed and after motion duly made, seconded and carried were approved. It was further resolved that the Board of Directors has determined that the consideration was valued at least equal to the value of the shares to be issued and that upon tender of the consideration, fully paid non-assessable shares of the corporation be issued.

There being no further business before the meeting, on motion duly made, seconded and carried, the meeting adjourned.

DATED: _____

_____
President

_____
Secretary

BYLAWS

OF

_____

ARTICLE I
OFFICES

Section 1.1 <u>Principal Office</u>: The principal office of the Corporation shall be located in the City of
_____ , County of _____ , State of Texas.

Section 1.2 <u>Other Offices</u>: The Corporation may also have offices at such other places, within or without the State of Texas, as the Board of Directors may from time to time determine, or as the business of the Corporation may require.

ARTICLE II
MEETINGS OF SHAREHOLDERS

Section 2.1 <u>Time and Place of Meetings</u>: All meetings of the shareholders shall be held at such time and place, within or without the State of Texas, as shall be stated in the notice of the meeting or in a duly executed waiver of notice thereof.

Section 2.2 <u>Annual Meetings</u>: Annual meetings of shareholders, commencing with the year _____ , shall be held on the _____ of _____ if not a legal holiday, and if a legal holiday, then on the next business day following, at 9:00 A.M., or at such other date and time as shall be designated from time to time by the Board of Directors and stated in the notice of the meeting. At the annual meeting, the shareholders entitled to vote thereat shall elect a Board of Directors and transact such other business as may properly be brought before the meeting.

Section 2.3 <u>Special Meetings</u>: Special meetings of the shareholders, unless otherwise prescribed by statute or provided by the Articles of Incorporation or these Bylaws, may be called by the President or the Board of Directors or by the holders of at least 10% of all shares entitled to vote at the meeting. Business conducted at any special meeting shall be confined to the purpose or purposes described in the notice thereof.

Section 2.4 <u>Notice</u>: Written or printed notice stating the place, day and hour of the meeting and, in the case of a special meeting, the purpose or purposes for which the meeting is called, shall be delivered not less than 10 calendar days (20 calendar days in the case of a meeting to approve a plan of merger or exchange) nor more than 60 calendar days before the date of the meeting, either personally or by mail, by or at the direction of the President, the Secretary or the officer or other person calling the meeting, to each shareholder of record entitled to vote at such meeting. If mailed, such notice shall be deemed to be delivered when deposited in the United States mail, addressed to the shareholder at his or its address as it appears on the share transfer records of the Corporation, with postage thereon prepaid.

Section 2.5 <u>Quorum; Withdrawal of Quorum</u>: A quorum shall be present at a meeting of shareholders if the holder or holders of a majority of the shares entitled to vote are present in person, represented by duly authorized representative in the case of a corporation or other legal entity or represented by proxy, unless otherwise provided in the Articles of Incorporation. Unless otherwise provided in the Articles of Incorporation or these Bylaws, once a quorum is present at a duly constituted meeting of shareholders, the shareholders present or represented at the meeting may conduct such business as may be properly brought before the meeting until it is adjourned, and the subsequent withdrawal from the meeting of any shareholder present or represented shall not affect the presence of a quorum at the meeting. Unless otherwise provided in the Articles of Incorporation or these Bylaws, the shareholders entitled to vote and present or represented at a meeting of shareholders at which a quorum is not present may adjourn the meeting until such time and to such place as may be determined by a vote of the holders of a majority of the shares represented at that meeting. At such adjourned meeting at which a quorum shall be present or represented, any business may be conducted which might have been conducted at the meeting as originally notified.

Section 2.6 <u>Voting</u>: With respect to any matter, other than the election of directors or a matter for which the affirmative vote of the holders of a specified portion of the shares is required by statute, the affirmative vote of the holders of a majority of the shares entitled to vote on that matter and represented at a meeting of shareholders at which a quorum is present shall be the act of the shareholders, unless otherwise provided in the Articles of Incorporation or these Bylaws. Unless otherwise provided in the Articles of Incorporation or these Bylaws, directors shall be elected by a plurality of the votes cast by the holders of shares entitled to vote in the election of directors at a meeting of shareholders at which a quorum is present.

Section 2.7 <u>Method of Voting</u>: Each outstanding share shall be entitled to one vote on each matter submitted to a vote at a meeting of shareholders, except to the extent that the Articles of Incorporation provide for more or less than one vote per share or limit or deny voting rights to the holders of the shares of any class or series or as otherwise provided by statute. A shareholder may vote in person, by duly authorized representative in the case of a corporation or other legal entity or by proxy executed in writing by the shareholder or by his or its duly authorized attorney-in-fact. Each proxy shall be filed with the Secretary of the Corporation prior to the time of the meeting.

Section 2.8 <u>Action Without Meeting</u>: Unless otherwise provided in the Articles of Incorporation, any action required or permitted to be taken at any meeting of the shareholders may be taken without a meeting, without prior notice and without a vote, if a consent or consents in writing, setting forth the action so taken, shall have been signed by the holder or holders of all the shares entitled to vote with respect to the action that is the subject of the consent.

ARTICLE III
DIRECTORS

Section 3.1 <u>Responsibilities</u>: The powers of the Corporation shall be exercised by or under the authority of, and the business and affairs of the Corporation shall be managed under the direction of, its Board of Directors.

Section 3.2 <u>Number; Election; Qualification; Term; Removal</u>: The Board of Directors shall consist of one or more members. The initial directors of the Corporation shall be as set forth in the original Articles of Incorporation. Thereafter, the number of directors shall be fixed from time to time by the Board of Directors or by the shareholders at the annual or a special meeting; provided, however, that no decrease in the number of directors shall have the effect of shortening the term of an incumbent director. The directors shall be elected at the annual meeting of the shareholders, except as provided in Section 3.3 below. At each annual meeting, the holders of shares entitled to vote in the election of directors shall elect directors to hold office until the next succeeding annual meeting. Unless removed in accordance with the Articles of Incorporation or this Section 3.2, each director elected shall hold office for the term for which he is elected and until his successor shall have been elected and qualified. Directors need not be residents of the State of Texas or shareholders of the Corporation. At any meeting of shareholders called expressly for that purpose, any director or the entire Board of Directors may be removed, with or without cause, by the affirmative vote of the holder or holders of a majority of the shares then entitled to vote at an election of directors.

Section 3.3 <u>Vacancies; Increases</u>: Any vacancy occurring in the Board of Directors (by death, resignation, removal or otherwise) may be filled by election at an annual or special meeting of shareholders called for that purpose, by the affirmative vote of a majority of the remaining directors then in office, though less than a quorum, or by a sole remaining director. Each director elected to fill a vacancy shall be elected for the unexpired term of his predecessor in office. Any directorship to be filled by reason of an increase in the number of directors may be filled by election at an annual or special meeting of shareholders called for that purpose or by the Board of Directors for a term of office continuing only until the next election of one or more directors by the shareholders; provided, however, that the Board of Directors may not fill more than two such directorships during the period between any two successive annual meetings of shareholders.

Section 3.4 <u>Place of Meetings</u>: Meetings of the Board of Directors, regular or special, may be held either within or without the State of Texas.

Section 3.5 <u>Regular Meetings</u>: Regular meetings of the Board of Directors may be held at such time and at such place as shall from time to time be determined by the Board of Directors. Regular meetings of the Board of Directors may be held without notice.

Section 3.6 <u>Special Meetings</u>: Special meetings of the Board of Directors may be called by the Chairman of the Board or by the President and shall be called by the Secretary on the written request of at least two directors. Written notice specifying the time and place of special meetings shall be given to each director at least three days before the date of the meeting. Such notice may, but need not, specify the purpose or purposes of the meeting.

Section 3.7 <u>Quorum; Majority Vote</u>: At all meetings, a majority of the number of the directors fixed in the manner provided in these Bylaws shall constitute a quorum for the transaction of business unless a greater number is specifically required by statute or provided in the Articles of Incorporation or these Bylaws. The act of a majority of the directors present at a meeting at which a quorum is present shall be the act of the Board of Directors, except as otherwise specifically required by statute or provided in the Articles of Incorporation or these Bylaws, in which case the express provision shall control. If a quorum shall not be present at any meeting of the Board of Directors, the directors present thereat may adjourn the meeting from time to time, without notice other than announcement at the meeting, until a quorum shall be present.

Section 3.8 <u>Minutes</u>: The Board of Directors shall keep regular minutes of its proceedings. The minutes shall be placed in the minute book of the Corporation.

Section 3.9 <u>Committees</u>: The Board of Directors, by resolution adopted by a majority of the full Board of Directors, may designate from among its members an executive committee and one or more other committees, each of which shall be comprised of one or more members, and may designate one or more of its members as alternate members of any committee, who may, subject to any limitations imposed by the Board of Directors, replace absent or disqualified members, at any meeting of that committee. Any such committee, to the extent provided in such resolution or in the Articles of Incorporation or these Bylaws, shall have and may exercise all of the authority of the Board of Directors, except as otherwise provided by statute. The designation of such committee and the delegation thereto of authority shall not operate to relieve the Board of Directors, or any member thereof, of any responsibility imposed by law. Such committee or committees shall have such name or names as may be determined from time to time by resolution adopted by the Board of Directors.

Section 3.10 <u>Committee Minutes</u>: Each committee shall keep regular minutes of its meetings and report the same to the Board of Directors when required. Such minutes shall be placed in the minute book of the Corporation.

Section 3.11 <u>Action Without Meeting</u>: Unless otherwise restricted by the Articles of Incorporation or these Bylaws, any action required or permitted to be taken at a meeting of the Board of Directors or any committee may be taken without a meeting if a consent in writing, setting forth the action so taken, is signed by all the members of the Board of Directors or committee, as the case may be. Such consent shall have the same force and effect as a unanimous vote at a meeting.

ARTICLE IV
NOTICES

Section 4.1 <u>Method</u>: Whenever by statute, the Articles of Incorporation, these Bylaws or otherwise, notice is required to be given to a director or shareholder, and no provision is made as to how the notice shall be given, it shall not be construed to be personal notice, but any such notice may be given: (a) in writing, by mail, postage prepaid, addressed to the director at the last address known by the Corporation for such director or shareholder at the address appearing on the share transfer records of the Corporation, or (b) in any other method permitted by law. Any notice required or permitted to be given by mail shall be deemed given at the time when the same is deposited in the United States mail.

Section 4.2 <u>Waiver</u>: Whenever by statute, the Articles of Incorporation or these Bylaws, any notice is required to be given to a director or shareholder, a waiver thereof in writing, signed by the person or persons entitled to such notice, or in the case of a corporation or other legal entity by its duly authorized representative, whether before or after the time stated therein, shall be equivalent to the giving of such notice.

ARTICLE V
OFFICERS

Section 5.1 <u>Number</u>: The officers of the Corporation shall consist of a President and a Secretary, each of whom shall be elected by the Board of Directors. The Board of Directors may also elect a Chairman of the Board, a Treasurer, a Controller and one or more Vice Presidents, Assistant Secretaries, Assistant Treasurers and Assistant Controllers. Any number of offices may be held by the same person.

Section 5.2 <u>Removal</u>: Any officer elected by the Board of Directors may be removed by the Board of Directors whenever in its judgment the best interests of the Corporation will be served thereby.

Section 5.3 <u>Compensation</u>: The compensation of all officers and agents of the Corporation who are also directors of the Corporation shall be fixed by the Board of Directors. The Board of Directors may delegate the power to fix the compensation of all other officers and agents of the Corporation to an officer of the Corporation.

Section 5.4 <u>Duties</u>: The officers of the Corporation shall have such authority and shall perform such duties as are customarily incident to their respective offices, or as may be specified from time to time by resolution of the Board of Directors regardless of whether such authority and duties are customarily incident to such office.

ARTICLE VI
INDEMNIFICATION OF DIRECTORS AND OFFICERS

Section 6.1 <u>Indemnification</u>: Each person who is or was a director, officer, employee or agent of the Corporation, or is or was serving at the request of the Corporation as a director, officer, partner, venturer, proprietor, trustee, employee, agent or similar functionary of another corporation, partnership, joint venture, sole proprietorship, trust or other enterprise or employee benefit plan (including the heirs, executors, administrators or estate of such person) shall be indemnified by the Corporation to the fullest extent that a corporation is required or permitted to grant indemnification to such person under the Texas Business Corporation Act, as the same exists or may hereafter be amended. Reasonable expenses incurred by a director, officer, employee or agent of the Corporation who was, is or is threatened to be made a named defendant or respondent in a proceeding shall be paid or reimbursed by the Corporation, in advance of the final disposition of the proceeding, to the maximum extent permitted under the Texas Business Corporation Act, as the same exists or may hereafter be amended. The right to indemnification under this Article VI shall be a contract right. In the event of the death of any person having a right of indemnification under this Article VI, such right will inure to the benefit of his or her heirs, executors, administrators and personal representatives. The rights under this Article VI will not be exclusive of any other right which any person may have or hereinafter acquire under any statute, bylaw, resolution of shareholders or directors, agreement or otherwise.

ARTICLE VII
CERTIFICATES REPRESENTING SHARES

Section 7.1 <u>Certificates</u>: The Corporation shall deliver certificates in the form approved by the Board of Directors representing all shares to which shareholders are entitled, and such certificates shall be signed by at least one officer of the Corporation, who shall be the Chairman of the Board, the President or a Vice President.

Section 7.2 <u>Lost, Stolen or Destroyed Certificates</u>: The Board of Directors may direct a new certificate or certificates to be issued in place of any certificate or certificates theretofore issued by the Corporation alleged to have been lost, stolen or destroyed, upon the making of an affidavit of that fact by the person claiming the certificate of stock to be lost, stolen or destroyed. When authorizing such issue of a new certificate or certificates, the Board of Directors may, in its discretion and as a condition precedent to the issuance thereof, require the owner of such lost, stolen or destroyed certificate or certificates, or his or its legal representative, to give the Corporation a bond, undertaking or other form of security in such sum and on such terms as it may reasonably direct as indemnity against any claim that may be made against the Corporation with respect to the certificate alleged to have been lost, stolen or destroyed.

Section 7.3 New Certificates: Upon surrender to the Corporation or the transfer agent of the Corporation of a certificate or certificates for shares duly endorsed or accompanied by proper evidence of succession, assignment or authority to transfer, it shall be the duty of the Corporation to issue a new certificate to the shareholder entitled thereto, cancel the old certificate, and record the transaction upon its books.

ARTICLE VIII
GENERAL PROVISIONS

Section 8.1 Distributions and Share Dividends: Subject to statute and any provision of the Articles of Incorporation, distributions (in the form of cash or property) or share dividends may be declared by the Board of Directors at any regular or special meeting.

Section 8.2 Checks: All checks, demands for money and notes of the Corporation shall be signed by such officer or officers or such other person or persons as the Board of Directors may from time to time designate.

Section 8.3 Fiscal Year: The fiscal year of the Corporation shall be fixed by resolution of the Board of Directors.

Section 8.4 Seal: The Board of Directors may adopt a corporate seal and use the same by causing it or a facsimile thereof to be impressed, affixed, reproduced or otherwise.

Section 8.5 Telephone and Similar Meetings: Unless otherwise restricted by the Articles of Incorporation or these Bylaws, the shareholders, members of the Board of Directors or members of any committee of the Board of Directors may participate in and hold a meeting of such shareholders, the Board of Directors or committee, as the case may be, by means of conference telephone or similar communications equipment by means of which all persons participating in the meeting can hear each other, and participation in such a meeting shall constitute presence in person at the meeting, except where a person participates in the meeting for the express purpose of objecting to the transaction of any business on the ground that the meeting is not lawfully called or convened.

Section 8.6 Amendment of Bylaws: Unless otherwise provided in the Texas Business Corporation Act, the Articles of Incorporation or these Bylaws, these Bylaws may be altered, amended or repealed, or new bylaws may be adopted, by the shareholders or the Board of Directors, subject to the shareholders providing in amending, repealing or adopting a particular Bylaw that it may not be amended or repealed by the Board of Directors.

BYLAWS

OF

_____

ARTICLE I
OFFICES

Section 1.1 <u>Principal Office</u>: The principal office of the Corporation shall be located in the City of _____,County of _____, State of Texas.

Section 1.2 <u>Other Offices</u>: The Corporation may also have offices at such other places, within or without the State of Texas, as the Board of Directors may from time to time determine, or as the business of the Corporation may require.

ARTICLE II
MEETINGS OF SHAREHOLDERS

Section 2.1 <u>Time and Place of Meetings</u>: All meetings of the shareholders shall be held at such time and place, within or without the State of Texas, as shall be stated in the notice of the meeting or in a duly executed waiver of notice thereof.

Section 2.2 <u>Annual Meetings</u>: Annual meetings of shareholders, commencing with the year _____, shall be held on the _____ of _____ if not a legal holiday, and if a legal holiday, then on the next business day following, at 9:00 A.M., or at such other date and time as shall be designated from time to time by the Board of Directors and stated in the notice of the meeting. At the annual meeting, the shareholders entitled to vote thereat shall elect a Board of Directors and transact such other business as may properly be brought before the meeting.

Section 2.3 <u>Special Meetings</u>: Special meetings of the shareholders, unless otherwise prescribed by statute or provided by the Articles of Incorporation or these Bylaws, may be called by the President or the Board of Directors or by the holders of at least 10% of all shares entitled to vote at the meeting. Business conducted at any special meeting shall be confined to the purpose or purposes described in the notice thereof.

Section 2.4 <u>Notice</u>: Written or printed notice stating the place, day and hour of the meeting and, in the case of a special meeting, the purpose or purposes for which the meeting is called, shall be delivered not less than 10 calendar days (20 calendar days in the case of a meeting to approve a plan of merger or exchange) nor more than 60 calendar days before the date of the meeting, either personally or by mail, by or at the direction of the President, the Secretary or the officer or other person calling the meeting, to each shareholder of record entitled to vote at such meeting. If mailed, such notice shall be deemed to be delivered when deposited in the United States mail, addressed to the shareholder at his or its address as it appears on the share transfer records of the Corporation, with postage thereon prepaid.

Section 2.5 <u>Quorum; Withdrawal of Quorum</u>: A quorum shall be present at a meeting of shareholders if the holder or holders of a majority of the shares entitled to vote are present in person, represented by duly authorized representative in the case of a corporation or other legal entity or represented by proxy, unless otherwise provided in the Articles of Incorporation. Unless otherwise provided in the Articles of Incorporation or these Bylaws, once a quorum is present at a duly constituted meeting of shareholders, the shareholders present or represented at the meeting may conduct such business as may be properly brought before the meeting until it is adjourned, and the subsequent withdrawal from the meeting of any shareholder present or represented shall not affect the presence of a quorum at the meeting. Unless otherwise provided in the Articles of Incorporation or these Bylaws, the shareholders entitled to vote and present or represented at a meeting of shareholders at which a quorum is not present may adjourn the meeting until such time and to such place as may be determined by a vote of the holders of a majority of the shares represented at that meeting. At such adjourned meeting at which a quorum shall be present or represented, any business may be conducted which might have been conducted at the meeting as originally notified.

Section 2.6 <u>Voting</u>: With respect to any matter, other than the election of directors or a matter for which the affirmative vote of the holders of a specified portion of the shares is required by statute, the affirmative vote of the holders of a majority of the shares entitled to vote on that matter and represented at a meeting of shareholders at which a quorum is present shall be the act of the shareholders, unless otherwise provided in the Articles of Incorporation or these Bylaws. Unless otherwise provided in the Articles of Incorporation or these Bylaws, directors shall be elected by a plurality of the votes cast by the holders of shares entitled to vote in the election of directors at a meeting of shareholders at which a quorum is present.

Section 2.7 <u>Method of Voting</u>: Each outstanding share shall be entitled to one vote on each matter submitted to a vote at a meeting of shareholders, except to the extent that the Articles of Incorporation provide for more or less than one vote per share or limit or deny voting rights to the holders of the shares of any class or series or as otherwise provided by statute. A shareholder may vote in person, by duly authorized representative in the case of a corporation or other legal entity or by proxy executed in writing by the shareholder or by his or its duly authorized attorney-in-fact. Each proxy shall be filed with the Secretary of the Corporation prior to the time of the meeting.

Section 2.8 <u>Action Without Meeting</u>: Unless otherwise provided in the Articles of Incorporation, any action required or permitted to be taken at any meeting of the shareholders may be taken without a meeting, without prior notice and without a vote, if a consent or consents in writing, setting forth the action so taken, shall have been signed by the holder or holders of all the shares entitled to vote with respect to the action that is the subject of the consent.

Section 2.9 <u>Qualification of Shareholders</u>. Only persons who are duly licensed or otherwise legally authorized to render the professional service for which the corporation was organized may be shareholders of the Corporation. Neither the Corporation nor the shareholders may transfer any shares to persons who are not duly licensed. If any shareholder shall become disqualified to practice the profession, such shareholder shall immediately sever all employment with the Corporation and shall terminate all financial interest in the Corporation immediately. the Corporation or a qualified person may purchase the shares of the disqualified shareholder.

ARTICLE III
DIRECTORS

Section 3.1 <u>Responsibilities</u>: The powers of the Corporation shall be exercised by or under the authority of, and the business and affairs of the Corporation shall be managed under the direction of, its Board of Directors.

Section 3.2 <u>Number; Election; Qualification; Term; Removal</u>: The Board of Directors shall consist of one or more members. The initial directors of the Corporation shall be as set forth in the original Articles of Incorporation. Thereafter, the number of directors shall be fixed from time to time by the Board of Directors or by the shareholders at the annual or a special meeting; provided, however, that no decrease in the number of directors shall have the effect of shortening the term of an incumbent director. The directors shall be elected at the annual meeting of the shareholders, except as provided in Section 3.3 below. At each annual meeting, the holders of shares entitled to vote in the election of directors shall elect directors to hold office until the next succeeding annual meeting. Unless removed in accordance with the Articles of Incorporation or this Section 3.2, each director elected shall hold office for the term for which he is elected and until his successor shall have been elected and qualified. Directors need not be residents of the State of Texas or shareholders of the Corporation. No person not duly licensed or otherwise duly authorized to render the professional service of the Corporation shall be a Director. At any meeting of shareholders called expressly for that purpose, any director or the entire Board of Directors may be removed, with or without cause, by the affirmative vote of the holder or holders of a majority of the shares then entitled to vote at an election of directors.

Section 3.3 Vacancies; Increases: Any vacancy occurring in the Board of Directors (by death, resignation, removal or otherwise) may be filled by election at an annual or special meeting of shareholders called for that purpose, by the affirmative vote of a majority of the remaining directors then in office, though less than a quorum, or by a sole remaining director. Each director elected to fill a vacancy shall be elected for the unexpired term of his predecessor in office. Any directorship to be filled by reason of an increase in the number of directors may be filled by election at an annual or special meeting of shareholders called for that purpose or by the Board of Directors for a term of office continuing only until the next election of one or more directors by the shareholders; provided, however, that the Board of Directors may not fill more than two such directorships during the period between any two successive annual meetings of shareholders.

Section 3.4 Place of Meetings: Meetings of the Board of Directors, regular or special, may be held either within or without the State of Texas.

Section 3.5 Regular Meetings: Regular meetings of the Board of Directors may be held at such time and at such place as shall from time to time be determined by the Board of Directors. Regular meetings of the Board of Directors may be held without notice.

Section 3.6 Special Meetings: Special meetings of the Board of Directors may be called by the Chairman of the Board or by the President and shall be called by the Secretary on the written request of at least two directors. Written notice specifying the time and place of special meetings shall be given to each director at least three days before the date of the meeting. Such notice may, but need not, specify the purpose or purposes of the meeting.

Section 3.7 Quorum; Majority Vote: At all meetings, a majority of the number of the directors fixed in the manner provided in these Bylaws shall constitute a quorum for the transaction of business unless a greater number is specifically required by statute or provided in the Articles of Incorporation or these Bylaws. The act of a majority of the directors present at a meeting at which a quorum is present shall be the act of the Board of Directors, except as otherwise specifically required by statute or provided in the Articles of Incorporation or these Bylaws, in which case the express provision shall control. If a quorum shall not be present at any meeting of the Board of Directors, the directors present thereat may adjourn the meeting from time to time, without notice other than announcement at the meeting, until a quorum shall be present.

Section 3.8 Minutes: The Board of Directors shall keep regular minutes of its proceedings. The minutes shall be placed in the minute book of the Corporation.

Section 3.9 Committees: The Board of Directors, by resolution adopted by a majority of the full Board of Directors, may designate from among its members an executive committee and one or more other committees, each of which shall be comprised of one or more members, and may designate one or more of its members as alternate members of any committee, who may, subject to any limitations imposed by the Board of Directors, replace absent or disqualified members, at any meeting of that committee. Any such committee, to the extent provided in such resolution or in the Articles of Incorporation or these Bylaws, shall have and may exercise all of the authority of the Board of Directors, except as otherwise provided by statute. The designation of such committee and the delegation thereto of authority shall not operate to relieve the Board of Directors, or any member thereof, of any responsibility imposed by law. Such committee or committees shall have such name or names as may be determined from time to time by resolution adopted by the Board of Directors.

Section 3.10 Committee Minutes: Each committee shall keep regular minutes of its meetings and report the same to the Board of Directors when required. Such minutes shall be placed in the minute book of the Corporation.

Section 3.11 Action Without Meeting: Unless otherwise restricted by the Articles of Incorporation or these Bylaws, any action required or permitted to be taken at a meeting of the Board of Directors or any committee may be taken without a meeting if a consent in writing, setting forth the action so taken, is signed by all the members of the Board of Directors or committee, as the case may be. Such consent shall have the same force and effect as a unanimous vote at a meeting.

ARTICLE IV
NOTICES

Section 4.1 <u>Method</u>: Whenever by statute, the Articles of Incorporation, these Bylaws or otherwise, notice is required to be given to a director or shareholder, and no provision is made as to how the notice shall be given, it shall not be construed to be personal notice, but any such notice may be given: (a) in writing, by mail, postage prepaid, addressed to the director at the last address known by the Corporation for such director or shareholder at the address appearing on the share transfer records of the Corporation, or (b) in any other method permitted by law. Any notice required or permitted to be given by mail shall be deemed given at the time when the same is deposited in the United States mail.

Section 4.2 <u>Waiver</u>: Whenever by statute, the Articles of Incorporation or these Bylaws, any notice is required to be given to a director or shareholder, a waiver thereof in writing, signed by the person or persons entitled to such notice, or in the case of a corporation or other legal entity by its duly authorized representative, whether before or after the time stated therein, shall be equivalent to the giving of such notice.

ARTICLE V
OFFICERS

Section 5.1 <u>Number and Qualifications</u>: The officers of the Corporation shall consist of a President and a Secretary, each of whom shall be elected by the Board of Directors. The Board of Directors may also elect a Chairman of the Board, a Treasurer, a Controller and one or more Vice Presidents, Assistant Secretaries, Assistant Treasurers and Assistant Controllers. Any number of offices may be held by the same person. No person not duly licensed or otherwise duly authorized to render the professional service of the Corporation may hold an office.

Section 5.2 <u>Removal</u>: Any officer elected by the Board of Directors may be removed by the Board of Directors whenever in its judgment the best interests of the Corporation will be served thereby.

Section 5.3 <u>Compensation</u>: The compensation of all officers and agents of the Corporation who are also directors of the Corporation shall be fixed by the Board of Directors. The Board of Directors may delegate the power to fix the compensation of all other officers and agents of the Corporation to an officer of the Corporation.

Section 5.4 <u>Duties</u>: The officers of the Corporation shall have such authority and shall perform such duties as are customarily incident to their respective offices, or as may be specified from time to time by resolution of the Board of Directors regardless of whether such authority and duties are customarily incident to such office.

ARTICLE VI
INDEMNIFICATION OF DIRECTORS AND OFFICERS

Section 6.1 <u>Indemnification</u>: Each person who is or was a director, officer, employee or agent of the Corporation, or is or was serving at the request of the Corporation as a director, officer, partner, venturer, proprietor, trustee, employee, agent or similar functionary of another corporation, partnership, joint venture, sole proprietorship, trust or other enterprise or employee benefit plan (including the heirs, executors, administrators or estate of such person) shall be indemnified by the Corporation to the fullest extent that a corporation is required or permitted to grant indemnification to such person under the Texas Business Corporation Act, as the same exists or may hereafter be amended. Reasonable expenses incurred by a director, officer, employee or agent of the Corporation who was, is or is threatened to be made a named defendant or respondent in a proceeding shall be paid or reimbursed by the Corporation, in advance of the final disposition of the proceeding, to the maximum extent permitted under the Texas Business Corporation Act, as the same exists or may hereafter be amended. The right to indemnification under this Article VI shall be a contract right. In the event of the death of any person having a right of indemnification under this Article VI, such right will inure to the benefit of his or her heirs, executors, administrators and personal representatives. The rights under this Article VI will not be exclusive of any other right which any person may have or hereinafter acquire under any statute, bylaw, resolution of shareholders or directors, agreement or otherwise.

ARTICLE VII
CERTIFICATES REPRESENTING SHARES

Section 7.1 <u>Certificates</u>: The Corporation shall deliver certificates in the form approved by the Board of Directors representing all shares to which shareholders are entitled, and such certificates shall be signed by at least one officer of the Corporation, who shall be the Chairman of the Board, the President or a Vice President.

Section 7.2 <u>Lost, Stolen or Destroyed Certificates</u>: The Board of Directors may direct a new certificate or certificates to be issued in place of any certificate or certificates theretofore issued by the Corporation alleged to have been lost, stolen or destroyed, upon the making of an affidavit of that fact by the person claiming the certificate of stock to be lost, stolen or destroyed. When authorizing such issue of a new certificate or certificates, the Board of Directors may, in its discretion and as a condition precedent to the issuance thereof, require the owner of such lost, stolen or destroyed certificate or certificates, or his or its legal representative, to give the Corporation a bond, undertaking or other form of security in such sum and on such terms as it may reasonably direct as indemnity against any claim that may be made against the Corporation with respect to the certificate alleged to have been lost, stolen or destroyed.

Section 7.3 <u>New Certificates</u>: Upon surrender to the Corporation or the transfer agent of the Corporation of a certificate or certificates for shares duly endorsed or accompanied by proper evidence of succession, assignment or authority to transfer, it shall be the duty of the Corporation to issue a new certificate to the shareholder entitled thereto, cancel the old certificate, and record the transaction upon its books.

ARTICLE VIII
GENERAL PROVISIONS

Section 8.1 <u>Distributions and Share Dividends</u>: Subject to statute and any provision of the Articles of Incorporation, distributions (in the form of cash or property) or share dividends may be declared by the Board of Directors at any regular or special meeting.

Section 8.2 <u>Checks</u>: All checks, demands for money and notes of the Corporation shall be signed by such officer or officers or such other person or persons as the Board of Directors may from time to time designate.

Section 8.3 <u>Fiscal Year</u>: The fiscal year of the Corporation shall be fixed by resolution of the Board of Directors.

Section 8.4 <u>Seal</u>: The Board of Directors may adopt a corporate seal and use the same by causing it or a facsimile thereof to be impressed, affixed, reproduced or otherwise.

Section 8.5 <u>Telephone and Similar Meetings</u>: Unless otherwise restricted by the Articles of Incorporation or these Bylaws, the shareholders, members of the Board of Directors or members of any committee of the Board of Directors may participate in and hold a meeting of such shareholders, the Board of Directors or committee, as the case may be, by means of conference telephone or similar communications equipment by means of which all persons participating in the meeting can hear each other, and participation in such a meeting shall constitute presence in person at the meeting, except where a person participates in the meeting for the express purpose of objecting to the transaction of any business on the ground that the meeting is not lawfully called or convened.

Section 8.6 <u>Amendment of Bylaws</u>: Unless otherwise provided in the Texas Business Corporation Act, the Articles of Incorporation or these Bylaws, these Bylaws may be altered, amended or repealed, or new bylaws may be adopted, by the shareholders or the Board of Directors, subject to the shareholders providing in amending, repealing or adopting a particular Bylaw that it may not be amended or repealed by the Board of Directors.

Banking Resolution of

_____

The undersigned, being the corporate secretary of the above corporation, hereby certifies that on the _____ day of _____, 19___ the Board of Directors of the corporation adopted the following resolution:

RESOLVED that the corporation open bank accounts with _____ _____ and that the officers of the corporation are authorized to take such action as is necessary to open such accounts; that the bank's printed form of resolution is hereby adopted and incorporated into these minutes by reference and shall be placed in the minute book; that any _____ of the following persons shall have signature authority over the account:

_____   _____

_____   _____

and that said resolution has not been modified or rescinded.

Date: _____

_____
Corporate Secretary

(Seal)

Offer to Purchase Stock

Date: _____

To the Board of Directors of

_____

The undersigned, hereby offers to purchase _____ shares of the _____ stock of your corporation at a total purchase price of _____.

Very truly yours,

_____

– –

Offer to Sell Stock
Pursuant to Sec. 1244 I.R.C.

Date: _____

To: _____

Dear

The corporation hereby offers to sell to you _____ shares of its common stock at a price of $_____ per share. These shares are issued pursuant to Section 1244 of the Internal Revenue Code,

Your signature below shall constitute an acceptance of our offer as of the date it is received by the corporation.

Very truly yours,

_____

By:_____

Accepted:

_____

Bill of Sale

The undersigned, in consideration of the issuance of _____ shares of common stock of _____, a Texas corporation, hereby grants, bargains, sells, transfers and delivers unto said corporation the following goods and chattels:

To have and to hold the same forever.

And the undersigned, their heirs, successors and administrators, covenant and warrant that they are the lawful owners of the said goods and chattels and that they are free from all encumbrances, that the undersigned have the right to sell this property and that they will warrant and defend the sale of said property against the lawful claims and demands of all persons.

IN WITNESS whereof the undersigned have executed this Bill of Sale this _____ day of _____19____.

_____

_____

_____

Form L. IRS Form 2553

| Form **2553** (Rev. September 1993) Department of the Treasury Internal Revenue Service | **Election by a Small Business Corporation** (Under section 1362 of the Internal Revenue Code) ▶ For Paperwork Reduction Act Notice, see page 1 of instructions. ▶ See separate instructions. | OMB No. 1545-0146 Expires 8-31-96 |

Notes: 1. *This election, to be an "S corporation," can be accepted only if all the tests are met under* **Who May Elect** *on page 1 of the instructions; all signatures in Parts I and III are originals (no photocopies); and the exact name and address of the corporation and other required form information are provided.*

2. *Do not file* **Form 1120S,** *U.S. Income Tax Return for an S Corporation, until you are notified that your election is accepted.*

Part I	**Election Information**

Please Type or Print	Name of corporation (see instructions)	**A** Employer identification number (EIN)
	Number, street, and room or suite no. (If a P.O. box, see instructions.)	**B** Date incorporated
	City or town, state, and ZIP code	**C** State of incorporation

D Election is to be effective for tax year beginning (month, day, year) . . . . ▶ / /

| **E** Name and title of officer or legal representative who the IRS may call for more information | **F** Telephone number of officer or legal representative ( ) |

G If the corporation changed its name or address after applying for the EIN shown in **A**, check this box . . . . ▶ ☐

H If this election takes effect for the first tax year the corporation exists, enter month, day, and year of the **earliest** of the following: (1) date the corporation first had shareholders, (2) date the corporation first had assets, or (3) date the corporation began doing business . . . . ▶ / /

I Selected tax year: Annual return will be filed for tax year ending (month and day) ▶ ....

If the tax year ends on any date other than December 31, except for an automatic 52-53-week tax year ending with reference to the month of December, you **must** complete Part II on the back. If the date you enter is the ending date of an automatic 52-53-week tax year, write "52-53-week year" to the right of the date. See Temporary Regulations section 1.441-2T(e)(3).

J Name and address of each shareholder, shareholder's spouse having a community property interest in the corporation's stock, and each tenant in common, joint tenant, and tenant by the entirety. (A husband and wife (and their estates) are counted as one shareholder in determining the number of shareholders without regard to the manner in which the stock is owned.)	**K** Shareholders' Consent Statement. Under penalties of perjury, we declare that we consent to the election of the above-named corporation to be an "S corporation" under section 1362(a) and that we have examined this consent statement, including accompanying schedules and statements, and to the best of our knowledge and belief, it is true, correct, and complete. (Shareholders sign and date below.)*		**L** Stock owned		**M** Social security number or employer identification number (see instructions)	**N** Shareholder's tax year ends (month and day)
	Signature	Date	Number of shares	Dates acquired		

*For this election to be valid, the consent of each shareholder, shareholder's spouse having a community property interest in the corporation's stock, and each tenant in common, joint tenant, and tenant by the entirety must either appear above or be attached to this form. (See instructions for Column K if a continuation sheet or a separate consent statement is needed.)

Under penalties of perjury, I declare that I have examined this election, including accompanying schedules and statements, and to the best of my knowledge and belief, it is true, correct, and complete.

Signature of officer ▶   Title ▶   Date ▶

See Parts II and III on back.   Cat. No. 18629R

Part II **Selection of Fiscal Tax Year (All corporations using this part must complete item O and one of items P, Q, or R.)**

O   Check the applicable box below to indicate whether the corporation is:

1. ☐   A new corporation adopting the tax year entered in item I, Part I.

2. ☐   An existing corporation retaining the tax year entered in item I, Part I.

3. ☐   An existing corporation changing to the tax year entered in item I, Part I.

P   Complete item P if the corporation is using the expeditious approval provisions of Revenue Procedure 87-32, 1987-2 C.B. 396, to request: **(1)** a natural business year (as defined in section 4.01(1) of Rev. Proc. 87-32), or **(2)** a year that satisfies the ownership tax year test in section 4.01(2) of Rev. Proc. 87-32. Check the applicable box below to indicate the representation statement the corporation is making as required under section 4 of Rev. Proc. 87-32.

1. Natural Business Year ▶ ☐   I represent that the corporation is retaining or changing to a tax year that coincides with its natural business year as defined in section 4.01(1) of Rev. Proc. 87-32 and as verified by its satisfaction of the requirements of section 4.02(1) of Rev. Proc. 87-32. In addition, if the corporation is changing to a natural business year as defined in section 4.01(1), I further represent that such tax year results in less deferral of income to the owners than the corporation's present tax year. I also represent that the corporation is not described in section 3.01(2) of Rev. Proc. 87-32. (See instructions for additional information that must be attached.)

2. Ownership Tax Year ▶ ☐   I represent that shareholders holding more than half of the shares of the stock (as of the first day of the tax year to which the request relates) of the corporation have the same tax year or are concurrently changing to the tax year that the corporation adopts, retains, or changes to per item I, Part I. I also represent that the corporation is not described in section 3.01(2) of Rev. Proc. 87-32.

Note: *If you do not use item P and the corporation wants a fiscal tax year, complete either item Q or R below. Item Q is used to request a fiscal tax year based on a business purpose and to make a back-up section 444 election. Item R is used to make a regular section 444 election.*

Q   Business Purpose—To request a fiscal tax year based on a business purpose, you must check box Q1 and pay a user fee. See instructions for details. You may also check box Q2 and/or box Q3.

1. Check here ▶ ☐   if the fiscal year entered in item I, Part I, is requested under the provisions of section 6.03 of Rev. Proc. 87-32. Attach to Form 2553 a statement showing the business purpose for the requested fiscal year. See instructions for additional information that must be attached.

2. Check here ▶ ☐   to show that the corporation intends to make a back-up section 444 election in the event the corporation's business purpose request is not approved by the IRS. (See instructions for more information.)

3. Check here ▶ ☐   to show that the corporation agrees to adopt or change to a tax year ending December 31 if necessary for the IRS to accept this election for S corporation status in the event: (1) the corporation's business purpose request is not approved and the corporation makes a back-up section 444 election, but is ultimately not qualified to make a section 444 election, or (2) the corporation's business purpose request is not approved and the corporation did not make a back-up section 444 election.

R   Section 444 Election—To make a section 444 election, you must check box R1 and you may also check box R2.

1. Check here ▶ ☐   to show the corporation will make, if qualified, a section 444 election to have the fiscal tax year shown in item I, Part I. To make the election, you must complete **Form 8716**, Election To Have a Tax Year Other Than a Required Tax Year, and either attach it to Form 2553 or file it separately.

2. Check here ▶ ☐   to show that the corporation agrees to adopt or change to a tax year ending December 31 if necessary for the IRS to accept this election for S corporation status in the event the corporation is ultimately not qualified to make a section 444 election.

Part III **Qualified Subchapter S Trust (QSST) Election Under Section 1361(d)(2)****

Income beneficiary's name and address	Social security number
Trust's name and address	Employer identification number

Date on which stock of the corporation was transferred to the trust (month, day, year) . . . . ▶   /   /

In order for the trust named above to be a QSST and thus a qualifying shareholder of the S corporation for which this Form 2553 is filed, I hereby make the election under section 1361(d)(2). Under penalties of perjury, I certify that the trust meets the definitional requirements of section 1361(d)(3) and that all other information provided in Part III is true, correct, and complete.

_____   _____
Signature of income beneficiary or signature and title of legal representative or other qualified person making the election   Date

**Use of Part III to make the QSST election may be made only if stock of the corporation has been transferred to the trust on or before the date on which the corporation makes its election to be an S corporation. The QSST election must be made and filed separately if stock of the corporation is transferred to the trust after the date on which the corporation makes the S election.

 Printed on recycled paper   *U.S. Government Printing Office: 1993 — 301-628/80216*

Department of the Treasury
Internal Revenue Service

Instructions for Form 2553
(Revised September 1993)
Election by a Small Business Corporation

Section references are to the Internal Revenue Code unless otherwise noted.

Paperwork Reduction Act Notice.—We ask for the information on this form to carry out the Internal Revenue laws of the United States. You are required to give us the information. We need it to ensure that you are complying with these laws and to allow us to figure and collect the right amount of tax.

The time needed to complete and file this form will vary depending on individual circumstances. The estimated average time is:

Recordkeeping	6 hr., 13 min.
Learning about the law or the form	2 hr., 59 min.
Preparing, copying, assembling, and sending the form to the IRS	3 hr., 13 min.

If you have comments concerning the accuracy of these time estimates or suggestions for making this form more simple, we would be happy to hear from you. You can write to both the **Internal Revenue Service,** Attention: Reports Clearance Officer, T:FP, Washington, DC 20224; and the **Office of Management and Budget,** Paperwork Reduction Project (1545-0146), Washington, DC 20503. **DO NOT** send the tax form to either of these offices. Instead, see **Where To File** below.

General Instructions

Purpose.—To elect to be an "S corporation," a corporation must file Form 2553. The election permits the income of the S corporation to be taxed to the shareholders of the corporation rather than to the corporation itself, except as provided in Subchapter S of the Code. For more information, get **Pub. 589,** Tax Information on S Corporations.

Who May Elect.—A corporation may elect to be an S corporation only if it meets **all** of the following tests:

1. It is a domestic corporation.

2. It has no more than 35 shareholders. A husband and wife (and their estates) are treated as one shareholder for this requirement. All other persons are treated as separate shareholders.

3. It has only individuals, estates, or certain trusts as shareholders. See the instructions for Part III regarding qualified subchapter S trusts.

4. It has no nonresident alien shareholders.

5. It has only one class of stock (disregarding differences in voting rights). Generally, a corporation is treated as having only one class of stock if all outstanding shares of the corporation's stock confer identical rights to distribution and liquidation

proceeds. See Regulations section 1.1361-1(l) for more details.

6. It is not one of the following ineligible corporations:

a. A corporation that owns 80% or more of the stock of another corporation, unless the other corporation has not begun business and has no gross income;

b. A bank or thrift institution;

c. An insurance company subject to tax under the special rules of Subchapter L of the Code;

d. A corporation that has elected to be treated as a possessions corporation under section 936; or

e. A domestic international sales corporation (DISC) or former DISC.

7. It has a permitted tax year as required by section 1378 or makes a section 444 election to have a tax year other than a permitted tax year. Section 1378 defines a permitted tax year as a tax year ending December 31, or any other tax year for which the corporation establishes a business purpose to the satisfaction of the IRS. See Part II for details on requesting a fiscal tax year based on a business purpose or on making a section 444 election.

8. Each shareholder consents as explained in the instructions for Column K.

See sections 1361, 1362, and 1378 for additional information on the above tests.

Where To File.—File this election with the Internal Revenue Service Center listed below.

If the corporation's principal business, office, or agency is located in	Use the following Internal Revenue Service Center address
New Jersey, New York (New York City and counties of Nassau, Rockland, Suffolk, and Westchester)	Holtsville, NY 00501
New York (all other counties), Connecticut, Maine, Massachusetts, New Hampshire, Rhode Island, Vermont	Andover, MA 05501
Illinois, Iowa, Minnesota, Missouri, Wisconsin	Kansas City, MO 64999
Delaware, District of Columbia, Maryland, Pennsylvania, Virginia	Philadelphia, PA 19255
Florida, Georgia, South Carolina	Atlanta, GA 39901
Indiana, Kentucky, Michigan, Ohio, West Virginia	Cincinnati, OH 45999
Kansas, New Mexico, Oklahoma, Texas	Austin, TX 73301
Alaska, Arizona, California (counties of Alpine, Amador, Butte, Calaveras, Colusa, Contra Costa, Del Norte, El Dorado, Glenn, Humboldt, Lake, Lassen, Marin, Mendocino, Modoc, Napa, Nevada, Placer, Plumas, Sacramento, San Joaquin, Shasta, Sierra, Siskiyou, Solano, Sonoma, Sutter, Tehama, Trinity, Yolo, and Yuba), Colorado, Idaho, Montana, Nebraska, Nevada, North Dakota, Oregon, South Dakota, Utah, Washington, Wyoming	Ogden, UT 84201
California (all other counties), Hawaii	Fresno, CA 93888
Alabama, Arkansas, Louisiana, Mississippi, North Carolina, Tennessee	Memphis, TN 37501

When To Make the Election.—Complete and file Form 2553 **(a)** at any time before the 16th day of the third month of the tax year, if filed during the tax year the election is to take effect, or **(b)** at any time during the preceding tax year. An election made no later than 2 months and 15 days after the beginning of a tax year that is less than 2½ months long is treated as timely made for that tax year. An election made after the 15th day of the third month but before the end of the tax year is effective for the next year. For example, if a calendar tax year corporation makes the election in April 1994, it is effective for the corporation's 1995 calendar tax year. See section 1362(b) for more information.

Acceptance or Nonacceptance of Election.—The Service Center will notify the corporation if its election is accepted and when it will take effect. The corporation will also be notified if its election is not accepted. The corporation should generally receive a determination on its election within 60 days after it has filed Form 2553. If box Q1 in Part II is checked on page 2, the corporation will receive a ruling letter from the IRS in Washington, DC, that either approves or denies the selected tax year. When box Q1 is checked, it will generally take an additional 90 days for the Form 2553 to be accepted.

Do not file Form 1120S until the corporation is notified that its election has been accepted. If the corporation is now required to file **Form 1120,** U.S. Corporation Income Tax Return, or any other applicable tax return, continue filing it until the election takes effect.

Care should be exercised to ensure that the IRS receives the election. If the corporation is not notified of acceptance or nonacceptance of its election within 3 months of date of filing (date mailed), or within 6 months if box Q1 is checked, please take follow-up action by corresponding with the Service Center where the corporation filed the election. If the IRS questions whether Form 2553 was filed, an acceptable proof of filing is: **(a)** certified or registered mail receipt (timely filed); **(b)** Form 2553 with accepted stamp; **(c)** Form 2553 with stamped IRS received date; or **(d)** IRS letter stating that Form 2553 has been accepted.

End of Election.— Once the election is made, it stays in effect for all years until it is terminated. During the 5 years after the election is terminated under section 1362(d), the corporation (or a successor corporation) can make another election on Form 2553 only with IRS consent. See Regulations section 1.1362-5 for more details.

Specific Instructions

Part I

Part I must be completed by all corporations.

Name and Address of Corporation.—Enter the true corporate name as set forth in the corporate charter or other legal document creating it. If the corporation's mailing address is the same as someone else's, such as a shareholder's, please enter "c/o" and this person's name following the name of the corporation. Include the suite, room, or other unit number after the street address. If the Post Office does not deliver to the street address and the corporation has a P.O. box, show the box number instead of the street address. If the corporation changed its name or address after applying for its EIN, be sure to check the box in item G of Part I.

Item A. Employer Identification Number.—If the corporation has applied for an employer identification number (EIN) but has not received it, enter "applied for." If the corporation does not have an EIN, it should apply for one on **Form SS-4**, Application for Employer Identification Number, available from most IRS and Social Security Administration offices.

Item D. Effective Date of Election.—Enter the beginning effective date (month, day, year) of the tax year requested for the S corporation. Generally, this will be the beginning date of the tax year for which the ending effective date is required to be shown in item I, Part I. For a new corporation (first year the corporation exists) it will generally be the date required to be shown in item H, Part I. The tax year of a new corporation starts on the date that it has shareholders, acquires assets, or begins doing business, whichever happens first. If the effective date for item D for a newly formed corporation is later than the date in item H, the corporation should file Form 1120 or Form 1120-A, for the tax period between these dates.

Column K. Shareholders' Consent Statement.—Each shareholder who owns (or is deemed to own) stock at the time the election is made must consent to the election. If the election is made during the corporation's tax year for which it first takes effect, any person who held stock at any time during the part of that year that occurs before the election is made, must consent to the election, even though the person may have sold or transferred his or her stock before the

election is made. Each shareholder consents by signing and dating in column K or signing and dating a separate consent statement described below.

An election made during the first 2½ months of the tax year is effective for the following tax year if any person who held stock in the corporation during the part of the tax year before the election was made, and who did not hold stock at the time the election was made, did not consent to the election.

If a husband and wife have a community interest in the stock or in the income from it, both must consent. Each tenant in common, joint tenant, and tenant by the entirety also must consent.

A minor's consent is made by the minor or the legal representative of the minor, or by a natural or adoptive parent of the minor if no legal representative has been appointed.

The consent of an estate is made by an executor or administrator.

If stock is owned by a trust that is a qualified shareholder, the deemed owner of the trust must consent. See section 1361(c)(2) for details regarding qualified trusts that may be shareholders and rules on determining who is the deemed owner of the trust.

Continuation sheet or separate consent statement.—If you need a continuation sheet or use a separate consent statement, attach it to Form 2553. The separate consent statement must contain the name, address, and employer identification number of the corporation and the shareholder information requested in columns J through N of Part I.

If you want, you may combine all the shareholders' consents in one statement.

Column L.—Enter the number of shares of stock each shareholder owns and the dates the stock was acquired. If the election is made during the corporation's tax year for which it first takes effect, do not list the shares of stock for those shareholders who sold or transferred all of their stock before the election was made. However, these shareholders must still consent to the election for it to be effective for the tax year.

Column M.—Enter the social security number of each shareholder who is an individual. Enter the employer identification number of each shareholder that is an estate or a qualified trust.

Column N.—Enter the month and day that each shareholder's tax year ends. If a shareholder is changing his or her tax year, enter the tax year the shareholder is changing to, and attach an explanation indicating the present tax year and the basis for the change (e.g., automatic revenue procedure or letter ruling request).

If the election is made during the corporation's tax year for which it first takes effect, you do not have to enter the tax year of any shareholder who sold or transferred all of his or her stock before the election was made.

Signature.—Form 2553 must be signed by the president, treasurer, assistant treasurer, chief accounting officer, or other corporate officer (such as tax officer) authorized to sign.

Part II

Complete Part II if you selected a tax year ending on any date other than December 31

(other than a 52-53-week tax year ending with reference to the month of December).

Box P1.—Attach a statement showing separately for each month the amount of gross receipts for the most recent 47 months as required by section 4.03(3) of Revenue Procedure 87-32, 1987-2 C.B. 396. A corporation that does not have a 47-month period of gross receipts cannot establish a natural business year under section 4.01(1).

Box Q1.—For examples of an acceptable business purpose for requesting a fiscal tax year, see Revenue Ruling 87-57, 1987-2 C.B. 117.

In addition to a statement showing the business purpose for the requested fiscal year, you must attach the other information necessary to meet the ruling request requirements of Revenue Procedure 93-1, 1993-1 I.R.B. 10 (updated annually). Also attach a statement that shows separately the amount of gross receipts from sales or services (and inventory costs, if applicable) for each of the 36 months preceding the effective date of the election to be an S corporation. If the corporation has been in existence for fewer than 36 months, submit figures for the period of existence.

If you check box Q1, you must also pay a user fee of $200 (subject to change). Do not pay the fee when filing Form 2553. The Service Center will send Form 2553 to the IRS in Washington, DC, who, in turn, will notify the corporation that the fee is due. See Revenue Procedure 93-23, 1993-19 I.R.B. 6.

Box Q2.—If the corporation makes a back-up section 444 election for which it is qualified, then the election must be exercised in the event the business purpose request is not approved. Under certain circumstances, the tax year requested under the back-up section 444 election may be different than the tax year requested under business purpose. See **Form 8716**, Election To Have a Tax Year Other Than a Required Tax Year, for details on making a back-up section 444 election.

Boxes Q2 and R2.—If the corporation is not qualified to make the section 444 election after making the item Q2 back-up section 444 election or indicating its intention to make the election in item R1, and therefore it later files a calendar year return, it should write "Section 444 Election Not Made" in the top left corner of the 1st calendar year Form 1120S it files.

Part III

Certain Qualified Subchapter S Trusts (QSSTs) may make the QSST election required by section 1361(d)(2) in Part III. Part III may be used to make the QSST election only if corporate stock has been transferred to the trust on or before the date on which the corporation makes its election to be an S corporation. However, a statement can be used in lieu of Part III to make the election.

Note: *Part III may be used only in conjunction with making the Part I election (i.e., Form 2553 cannot be filed with only Part III completed).*

The deemed owner of the QSST must also consent to the S corporation election in column K, page 1, of Form 2553. See section 1361(c)(2).

Printed on recycled paper

*U.S. Government Printing Office: 1993 — 301-628/80221

Resolution
of

_____

a Texas Corporation

RESOLVED that the corporation elects "S-corporation" status for tax purposes under the Internal Revenue Code and that the officers of the corporation are directed to file IRS Form 2553 and to take any further action necessary for the corporation to qualify for S-corporation status.

Shareholders' Consent

The undersigned shareholders, being all of the shareholders of the above corporation, a Texas corporation, hereby consent to the election of the corporation to obtain S-corporation status

Name and Address of Shareholder	Shares Owned	Date Acquired
_____	_____	_____
_____		
_____	_____	_____
_____		
_____	_____	_____
_____		
_____	_____	_____
_____		
_____		

Date:_____

SHAREHOLDERS SIGNATURES

_____

_____

_____

_____

_____

WAIVER OF NOTICE OF THE ANNUAL MEETING OF
THE BOARD OF DIRECTORS OF

_____

The undersigned, being all the Directors of the corporation, hereby agree and consent that an annual meeting of the Board of Directors of the corporation be held on the _____ day of _____, 19___ at ___ o'clock ___m at _____ _____ and do hereby waive all notice whatsoever of such meeting and of any adjournment or adjournments thereof.

We do further agree and consent that any and all lawful business may be transacted at such meeting or at any adjournment or adjournments thereof as may be deemed advisable by the Directors present. Any business transacted at such meeting or at any adjournment or adjournments thereof shall be as valid and legal as if such meeting or adjourned meeting were held after notice.

Date: _____

_____
Director

_____
Director

_____
Director

_____
Director

MINITES OF THE ANNUAL MEETING OF
THE BOARD OF DIRECTORS OF

_____

   The annual meeting of the Board of Directors of the corporation was held on the date and at the time and place set forth in the written waiver of notice signed by the Board of Directors, and attached to the minutes of this meeting.

   The following were present, being all the Directors of the corporation:

_____   _____

_____   _____

   The meeting was called to order and it was moved, seconded and unanimously carried that _____ act as Chairman and that _____ act as Secretary.

   The minutes of the last meeting of the Board of Directors which was held on _____, 19___ were read and approved by the Board.

   Upon motion duly made, seconded and carried, the following were elected officers for the following year and until their successors are elected and qualify:

   President:
   Vice President:
   Secretary
   Treasurer:

   There being no further business to come before the meeting, upon motion duly made, seconded and unanimously carried, it was adjourned.

                              _____
                              Secretary

Directors:

_____

_____

_____

_____

WAIVER OF NOTICE OF THE ANNUAL MEETING OF
THE SHAREHOLDERS OF

_____

The undersigned, being all the shareholders of the corporation, hereby agree and consent that an annual meeting of the shareholders of the corporation be held on the ____ day of _____, 19___ at ___ o'clock __m at _____ _____ and do hereby waive all notice whatsoever of such meeting and of any adjournment or adjournments thereof.

We do further agree and consent that any and all lawful business may be transacted at such meeting or at any adjournment or adjournments thereof. Any business transacted at such meeting or at any adjournment or adjournments thereof shall be as valid and legal as if such meeting or adjourned meeting were held after notice.

Date: _____

_____
Shareholder

_____
Shareholder

_____
Shareholder

_____
Shareholder

MINUTES OF THE ANNUAL MEETING OF
SHAREHOLDERS OF

_____

The annual meeting of shareholders of the corporation was held on the date and at the time and place set forth in the written waiver of notice signed by the shareholders, and attached to the minutes of this meeting.

There were present the following shareholders:

Shareholder   No. of Shares

_____   _____
_____   _____
_____   _____
_____   _____

The meeting was called to order and it was moved, seconded and unanimously carried that _____ act as Chairman and that _____ act as Secretary.

A roll call was taken and the Chairman noted that all of the outstanding shares of the corporation were represented in person or by proxy. Any proxies were attached to these minutes.

The minutes of the last meeting of the shareholders which was held on _____, 19___ were read and approved by the shareholders.

Upon motion duly made, seconded and carried, the following were elected directors for the following year:

_____   _____
_____   _____

There being no further business to come before the meeting, upon motion duly made, seconded and unanimously carried, it was adjourned.

_____
Secretary

Shareholders:

_____

_____

_____

_____

119

WAIVER OF NOTICE OF SPECIAL MEETING OF
THE BOARD OF DIRECTORS OF

_____

The undersigned, being all the Directors of the corporation, hereby agree and consent that a special meeting of the Board of Directors of the Corporation be held on the ____ day of _____, 19___ at ___ o'clock __m at _____ _____ and do hereby waive all notice whatsoever of such meeting and of any adjournment or adjournments thereof.

The purpose of the meeting is:

We do further agree and consent that any and all lawful business may be transacted at such meeting or at any adjournment or adjournments thereof as may be deemed advisable by the Directors present. Any business transacted at such meeting or at any adjournment or adjournments thereof shall be as valid and legal as if such meeting or adjourned meeting were held after notice.

Date: _____

_____
Director

_____
Director

_____
Director

_____
Director

MINUTES OF SPECIAL MEETING OF
THE BOARD OF DIRECTORS OF

_____

A special meeting of the Board of Directors of the corporation was held on the date and at the time and place set forth in the written waiver of notice signed by the directors, and attached to the minutes of this meeting.

The following were present, being all the Directors of the corporation:

_____   _____

_____   _____

The meeting was called to order and it was moved, seconded and unanimously carried that _____ act as Chairman and that _____ act as Secretary.

The minutes of the last meeting of the Board of Directors which was held on _____, 19___ were read and approved by the Board.

Upon motion duly made, seconded and carried, the following resolution was adopted:

There being no further business to come before the meeting, upon motion duly made, seconded and unanimously carried, it was adjourned.

_____
Secretary

Directors:

_____

_____

_____

_____

WAIVER OF NOTICE OF SPECIAL MEETING OF
THE SHAREHOLDERS OF

_____

The undersigned, being all the shareholders of the corporation, hereby agree and consent that a special meeting of the shareholders of the corporation be held on the ____ day of _____, 19___ at ___ o'clock __m at _____ _____ and do hereby waive all notice whatsoever of such meeting and of any adjournment or adjournments thereof.

The purpose of the meeting is:

We do further agree and consent that any and all lawful business may be transacted at such meeting or at any adjournment or adjournments thereof. Any business transacted at such meeting or at any adjournment or adjournments thereof shall be as valid and legal as if such meeting or adjourned meeting were held after notice.

Date: _____

_____
Shareholder

_____
Shareholder

_____
Shareholder

_____
Shareholder

MINUTES OF SPECIAL MEETING OF
SHAREHOLDERS OF

_____

A special meeting of shareholders of the corporation was held on the date and at the time and place set forth in the written waiver of notice signed by the shareholders, and attached to the minutes of this meeting.

There were present the following shareholders:

Shareholder   No. of Shares

_____   _____
_____   _____
_____   _____
_____   _____

The meeting was called to order and it was moved, seconded and unanimously carried that _____ act as Chairman and that _____ act as Secretary.

A roll call was taken and the Chairman noted that all of the outstanding shares of the corporation were represented in person or by proxy. Any proxies were attached to these minutes.

The minutes of the last meeting of the shareholders which was held on _____, 19___ were read and approved by the shareholders.

Upon motion duly made, seconded and carried, the following resolution was adopted:

There being no further business to come before the meeting, upon motion duly made, seconded and unanimously carried, it was adjourned.

_____
Secretary

Shareholders:

_____

_____

_____

_____

Change of Registered Agent and/or Registered Office

1.   The name of the corporation is:

2.   The corporation charter number is:

3.   The street address of the PRESENT registered office is:

4.   The NEW address of the registered office is to be:

5.   The PRESENT registered agent is:

6.   The NEW registered agent is:

7.   The street address of the registered office and the street address of the office of the registered agent are identical.

8.   Such change was authorized by resolution duly adopted by the Board of Directors of the corporation or by an officer of the corporation so authorized by the Board of Directors.

_____
An Authorized Officer

Stock Ledger

Certificates Issued

Cert. No.	No. of Shares	Date of Acquisition	Shareholder Name and Address	From Whom Transferred	Amount Paid

Transfer of Shares

Date of Transfer	To Whom Transferred	Cert. No. Surrendered	No. of Shares Transferred	Cert. No.

Stub 1

Certificate No. _____
No. of shares _____
Dated _____
Issued to: _____

☐ Original issue
Documentary stamp tax paid:
$ _____
(Attach stamps to this stub.)

☐ Transferred from:
_____
Date: _____

Original Cert. No.	Original No. Shares	No. of Shares Transferred
_____	_____	_____

Received Cert. No. _____
No. of shares _____
New certificates issued:

Cert. No.	No. of Shares
_____	_____
_____	_____

Stub 2

Certificate No. _____
No. of shares _____
Dated _____
Issued to: _____

☐ Original issue
Documentary stamp tax paid:
$ _____
(Attach stamps to this stub.)

☐ Transferred from:
_____
Date: _____

Original Cert. No.	Original No. Shares	No. of Shares Transferred
_____	_____	_____

Received Cert. No. _____
No. of shares _____
New certificates issued:

Cert. No.	No. of Shares
_____	_____
_____	_____

Stub 3

Certificate No. _____
No. of shares _____
Dated _____
Issued to: _____

☐ Original issue
Documentary stamp tax paid:
$ _____
(Attach stamps to this stub.)

☐ Transferred from:
_____
Date: _____

Original Cert. No.	Original No. Shares	No. of Shares Transferred
_____	_____	_____

Received Cert. No. _____
No. of shares _____
New certificates issued:

Cert. No.	No. of Shares
_____	_____
_____	_____

Stub 1

Certificate No. _____
No. of shares _____
Dated _____
Issued to: _____

☐ Original issue
Documentary stamp tax paid:
$ _____
(Attach stamps to this stub.)

☐ Transferred from:
_____
Date: _____

Original Cert. No.	Original No. Shares	No. of Shares Transferred

Received Cert. No. _____
No. of shares _____
New certificates issued:

Cert. No.	No. of Shares

Stub 2

Certificate No. _____
No. of shares _____
Dated _____
Issued to: _____

☐ Original issue
Documentary stamp tax paid:
$ _____
(Attach stamps to this stub.)

☐ Transferred from:
_____
Date: _____

Original Cert. No.	Original No. Shares	No. of Shares Transferred

Received Cert. No. _____
No. of shares _____
New certificates issued:

Cert. No.	No. of Shares

Stub 3

Certificate No. _____
No. of shares _____
Dated _____
Issued to: _____

☐ Original issue
Documentary stamp tax paid:
$ _____
(Attach stamps to this stub.)

☐ Transferred from:
_____
Date: _____

Original Cert. No.	Original No. Shares	No. of Shares Transferred

Received Cert. No. _____
No. of shares _____
New certificates issued:

Cert. No.	No. of Shares

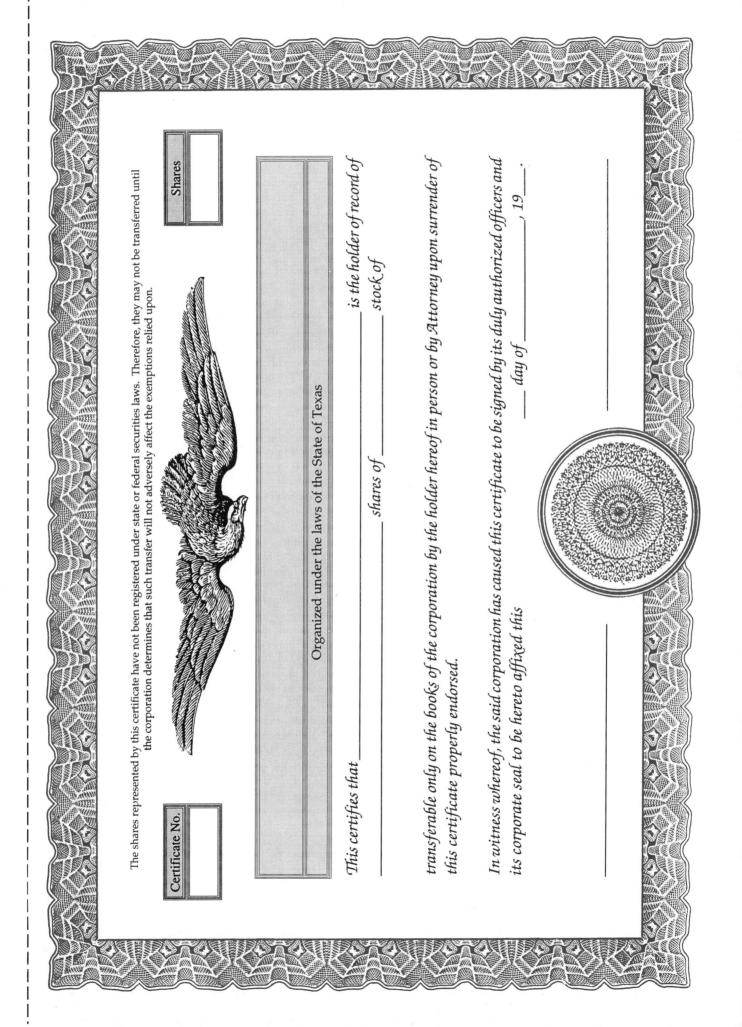

For value received, _____ hereby sell, assign and transfer unto _____

_____

_____

represented by this certificate and do hereby irrevocably constitute and appoint _____ *attorney to transfer the said shares on the books of the corporation with full power of substitution in the premises.*

Dated _____

_____

Witness:

_____

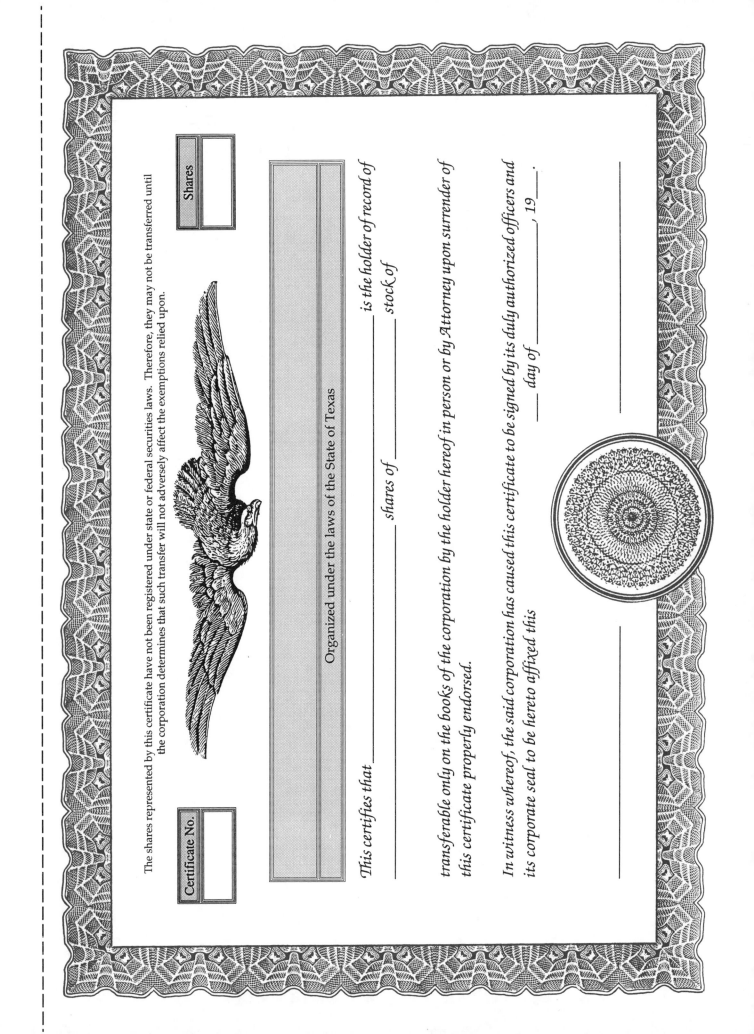

The shares represented by this certificate have not been registered under state or federal securities laws. Therefore, they may not be transferred until the corporation determines that such transfer will not adversely affect the exemptions relied upon.

Shares

Certificate No.

Organized under the laws of the State of Texas

This certifies that _____ is the holder of record of

_____ shares of _____ stock of

transferable only on the books of the corporation by the holder hereof in person or by Attorney upon surrender of this certificate properly endorsed.

In witness whereof, the said corporation has caused this certificate to be signed by its duly authorized officers and its corporate seal to be hereto affixed this _____ day of _____, 19____.

_____

_____

For value received, _____ hereby sell, assign and transfer unto _____

_____

_____

represented by this certificate and do hereby irrevocably constitute and appoint _____ *attorney to transfer the said shares on the books of the corporation with full power of substitution in the premises.*

Dated _____

_____

Witness:

_____

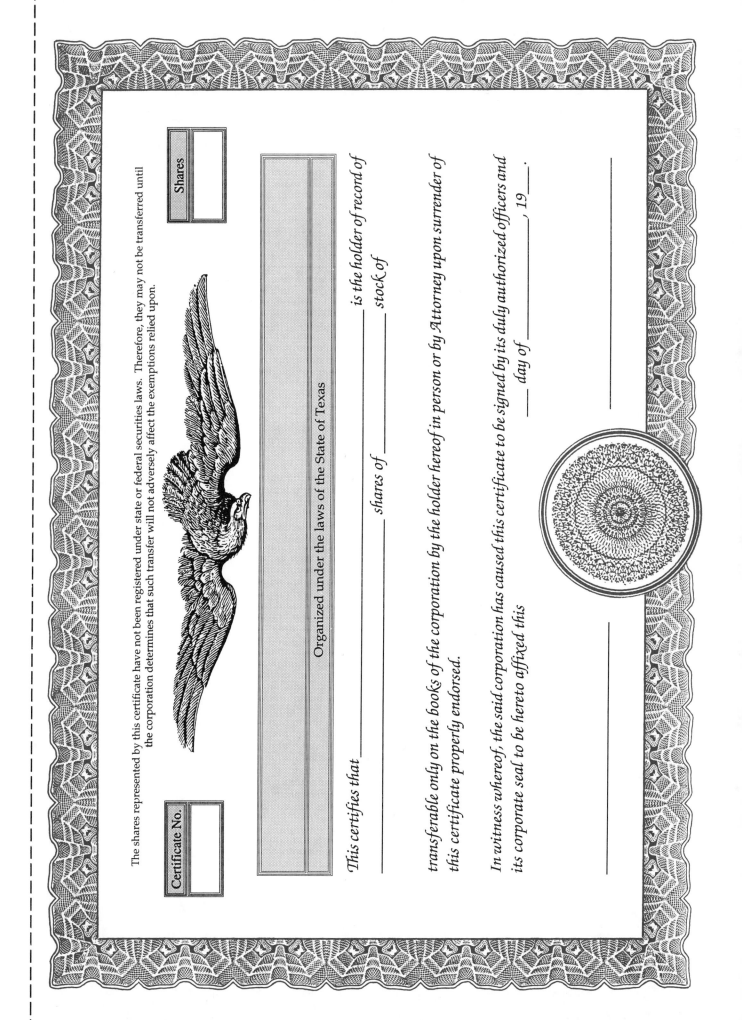

Shares

Certificate No.

The shares represented by this certificate have not been registered under state or federal securities laws. Therefore, they may not be transferred until the corporation determines that such transfer will not adversely affect the exemptions relied upon.

Organized under the laws of the State of Texas

This certifies that _____ is the holder of record of

_____ shares of _____ stock of

transferable only on the books of the corporation by the holder hereof in person or by Attorney upon surrender of this certificate properly endorsed.

In witness whereof, the said corporation has caused this certificate to be signed by its duly authorized officers and its corporate seal to be hereto affixed this _____ day of _____, 19____ .

_____   _____

For value received, _____ hereby sell, assign and transfer unto _____

_____

_____

represented   by   this   certificate   and   do   hereby   irrevocably   constitute   and   appoint
_____ *attorney to transfer the said shares on*
the   books   of   the   corporation   with   full   power   of   substitution   in   the   premises.

Dated _____

_____

Witness:

_____

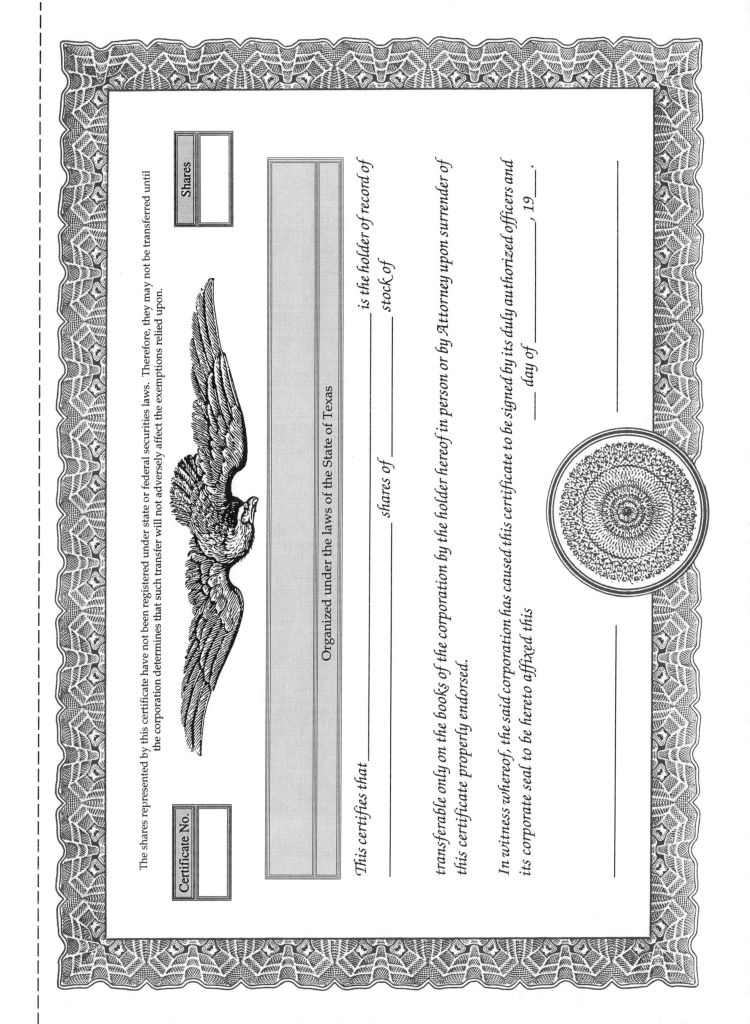

For value received, _____ hereby sell, assign and transfer unto _____

_____

_____

represented by this certificate and do hereby irrevocably constitute and appoint _____ *attorney to transfer the said shares on the books of the corporation with full power of substitution in the premises.*

Dated _____

_____

Witness:

_____

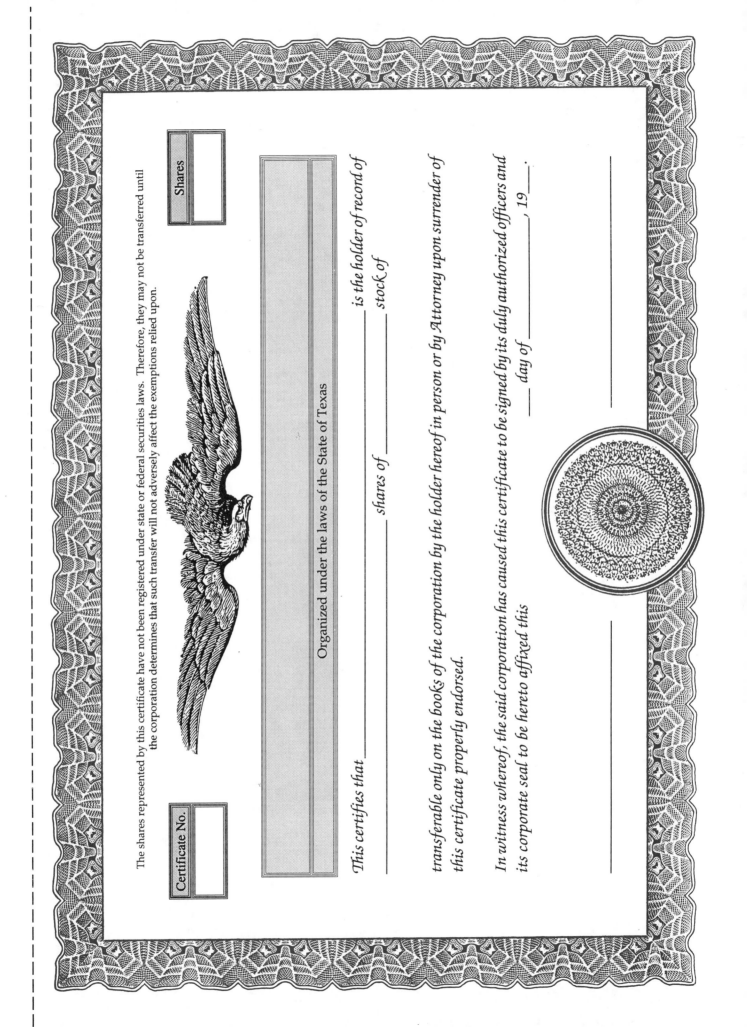

Certificate No.

Shares

The shares represented by this certificate have not been registered under state or federal securities laws. Therefore, they may not be transferred until the corporation determines that such transfer will not adversely affect the exemptions relied upon.

Organized under the laws of the State of Texas

This certifies that _____ is the holder of record of

_____ shares of _____ stock of

transferable only on the books of the corporation by the holder hereof in person or by Attorney upon surrender of this certificate properly endorsed.

In witness whereof, the said corporation has caused this certificate to be signed by its duly authorized officers and its corporate seal to be hereto affixed this _____ day of _____, 19 _____.

For value received, _____ *hereby sell, assign and transfer unto* _____

_____

represented by this certificate and do hereby irrevocably constitute and appoint _____ *attorney to transfer the said shares on the books of the corporation with full power of substitution in the premises.*

Dated _____

_____

Witness:

_____

Index

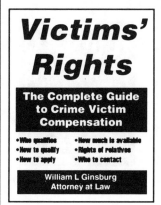
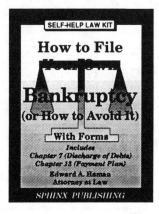

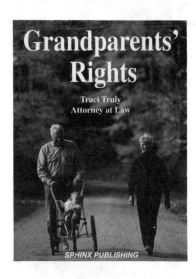
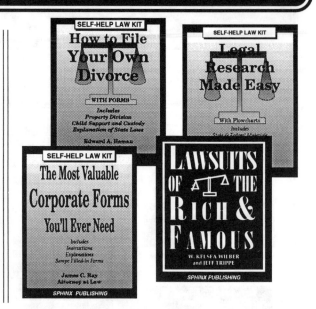

Self-Help Law for T E X A S

How to File for Divorce in Texas
By Karen Ann Rolcik & Edward A. Haman
ISBN 0-913825-91-3; 8 ½ x 11; 130 pages; $19.95
This book provides all of the information, forms and instructions for obtaining a divorce in Texas without a lawyer.

How to Make a Texas Will
By Karen Ann Rolcik & Mark Warda
ISBN 0-913825-89-1 ; 8 ½ x 11; 90 pages ; $9.95
This book explains Texas law regarding wills, inheritance laws, and joint property; includes 14 ready-to-use forms.

How to Start a Business in Texas
By William R. Brown & Mark Warda
ISBN 0-913825-90-5; 8 ½ x 11; 120 pages; $16.95
This book covers such important matters as licensing, sales tax collections, name registration, unemployment taxes, regulatory laws, worker compensation laws, advertising rules, labor laws, and taxes.

How to Form a Simple Corporation in Texas
By Karen Ann Rolcik & Mark Warda
ISBN 0-913825-009-2; 8 ½ x 11; 130 pages; $19.95
This book helps new business owners save precious capital by forming their own corporation with the expense of a lawyer. It includes forms with instructions.

How to Probate an Estate in Texas
By Karen Ann Rolcik
ISBN 0-913825-010-6 ; 8 ½ x 11; 124 pages ; $19.95
This book makes the Texas probate process understandable, with forms and instructions for the various types of probate.

How to Win in Small Claims Court in Texas
By William R. Brown & Mark Warda
ISBN 0-913825-012-2; 8 ½ x 11; 124 pages; $14.95
With the information, forms and instructions in this book, anyone with a claim up to $5,000 can bring their own lawsuit in Texas Small Claims Court.

Landlords' Rights and Duties in Texas
By William R. Brown & Mark Warda
ISBN 0-913825-011-4; 8 ½ x 11; 130 pages; $19.95
For both residential and commercial landlords, this book covers the law from the tenant's application to evictions and claims on security deposits.

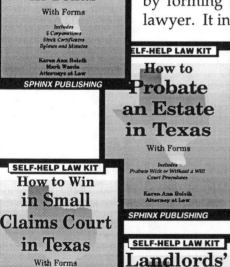

Books from other publishers

Represent Yourself in Court A step-by-step guide to preparing and trying a civil lawsuit. $29.95

Patent It Yourself, 3rd Ed. Explains every step of the patent process; a complete legal guide for inventors. $39.95

The Inventor's Notebook How to develop, document, protect, finance, and market your invention. $19.95

Plan Your Estate, 3rd Ed. For estates under $600,000, with specific instructions for preparing a living trust. $24.95

Make Your Own Living Trust For estates between $600,000 and $1,200,000. $19.95

How to Win Your Personal Injury Claim How to settle an injury claim on your own. $24.95

Beat the Nursing Home Trap: A Consumer's Guide to Choosing and Financing Long-Term Care $18.95
Explains how to choose and pay for long-term care, while protecting and conserving assets.

Social Security, Medicare & Pensions: The Sourcebook for Older Americans $18.95

The Living Together Kit, 7th Ed. Includes estate planning, living together agreements, buying real estate, etc. $24.95

Simple Contracts for Personal Use, 2nd Ed. Clearly written legal form contracts for all ocassions. $16.95

Stand Up to the IRS, 2nd Ed. Know your rights when dealing with IRS. $21.95

The Independent Paralegal's Handbook, 3rd Ed. $29.95
How to go into business helping consumers prepare their own paperwork in routine legal matters.

How to Write a Business Plan, 4th Ed. Finance your business and make it work. $21.95

A Legal Guide for Lesbian and Gay Couples, 8th Ed. $24.95
A practical guide covering living together, children, medical emergencies, estate planning, and more.

Your Rights in the Workplace: A Complete Guide for Employees, 2nd Ed. $15.95
Hiring, firing, wages, hours, family & medical leave, benefits, health & safety, discrimination, and more.

Sexual Harassment on the Job, 2nd Ed. Explains the rights of employees who are sexually harassed. $18.95

Order Form

To order these publications, please fill in the information requested and send check or money order to Sphinx Publishing, PO Box 25, Clearwater, FL 34617 or call 800-226-5291.

☐ Check Enclosed ☐ Money Order

We accept Visa, MasterCard, American Express and Discover cards.

Card number:

☐☐☐☐☐☐☐☐☐☐☐☐☐☐☐☐

Expiration date:

☐☐☐   ☐ American Express ☐ Visa
      ☐ MasterCard   ☐ Discover

Ship to:

Name_____

Address _____

City_____State_____

Zip_____ Phone_____

To order by credit card call:

1-800-226-5291

Or fax this form to (813) 586-5088

Quantity	Title	Price	Total Price

*Shipping: **In Florida:** UPS: (1-3 books) $3.25, each add'l .50¢
          4th class mail: (1 book) $1.50 , each add'l. 50¢
   [NOTE: Books from other publishers are only sent UPS]
Other States: UPS: (1-3 books) $3.75, each add'l .50¢

Subtotal: $_____
Sales Tax (FL residents) $_____
*Shipping: $_____
Total: $_____

Prices subject to change

_____
Signature